50 Groundbreaking Roller Coasters

Roller Coasters

The Most Important Scream Machines Ever Built

Nick Weisenberger

Copyright Information

Your Free Bonus

As a way of saying thanks for your purchase, I'm offering a free bonus gift that's exclusive to my book and blog readers. Theme parks and roller coasters are fun – waiting in long lines is not. If you want to save precious time during your amusement park visit you'll need to steer clear of those long queues. I've included my best advice to avoid wasting hours of your day by standing in line for one of these groundbreaking roller coasters this summer in an action-packed pdf. You can download this free resource at:

<u>http://www.thrillingbooks.net/FREE</u>

Table of Contents

Evolution of the Roller Coaster

Roller coasters are sophisticated systems that are a thousand technical miles beyond the Russian ice slides they evolved from. The amusement industry has entered an era of high-tech engineering. Higher speeds, higher loads (both structural and biomechanical), faster acceleration, crazy inversions, cantilevered seats, spinning cars—the designs are becoming increasingly more complex. Whether it is a deliberately shaky, wooden ride or a corkscrewing demon with your legs dangling in mid-air, every midway monster is a complex three-dimensional puzzle to be solved by engineers. *50 Groundbreaking Roller Coasters* is a comprehensive list of the most influential scream machines that drove the evolution of the modern roller coaster.

So what's the definition of a "roller coaster?" Anything at an amusement park that makes you scream your head off, right? Not according to the coaster boys. A roller coaster is defined as a passenger-carrying vehicle that rolls along one or more rails primarily due to gravity. The track does not necessarily have to be a complete, closed circuit. By this definition, "water slide coasters" (water slides that use rafts) are not included, but "water coasters" that run on tubular steel rails are on this list. Other extreme amusement park rides such as freefall drop towers, water slides, swing rides, alpine coasters, etc., are not included.

The ancestor of the modern roller coaster is thought to have originated in Russia in the 15th century, in the form of slides constructed of wood and covered in ice. These "Russian Mountains" were built to keep the local residents entertained during the long Russian winters. Over time, the ices slides became more and more sophisticated, and grew to be as tall as 70 feet. Sand was used at the end of the ramps to slow the sleds down. Originally, these early thrill rides could only be experienced during winter. But at the start of the 1800s, wheels were added to the sleds, enabling year-round rides. Interestingly enough, these roller coasters are translated from Russian as "American Mountains."

The next major advancement in the evolution of the roller coaster came in the early 1800s in France, when carts with wheels were first used on grooved tracks, which prevented the carts from flying off. Next, primitive cable systems were introduced to pull the carts to the top of the hills. Scenic railways appeared in America in the 1870s as a method for railroad companies to increase their business. Even more improvements were made, such as automatic lifts to the top of the tallest hill, wheels on the underside to lock the cars to the track, and two side-by-side rides that raced one another. But we'll get back to those later, when we look at the modern coasters they evolved into.

What makes a majority of the roller coasters listed in this book even more impressive is the fact that they were designed using pencil and paper rather than computers. Modern roller coasters are designed using the latest in computer technology. What used to be done with paper, pencil, and drawing boards is now done on a computer. The universal tool for the modern engineer is computer aided design (CAD) software. Changes and iterations are made on a computer in seconds. Programs such as AutoCAD are used to draft, adjust, and detail designs in accordance with ride standards. 3D CAD software, such as CATIA, SolidWorks, or AutoDesk Inventor, allow designers to store every step in the roller coaster design process within one computer program, including:

- ❖ 3D modeling
- ❖ 2D manufacturing drawings
- ❖ Kinematic simulations
- ❖ Finite element stress analysis (FEA)
- ❖ Seismic analysis of fixed or isolated structures
- ❖ High-resolution image renderings for marketing and sales purposes

Contemporary coasters are built to the highest standards, quality, and tolerances. Modern 3D CAD systems help engineers design rides within the limits of the biodynamic tolerances of passengers. A simulation of the coaster, based on the CAD data, can illustrate the g-forces and dynamic behavior of a ride long before a prototype has been built. The roller coaster is virtually assembled early in the design phase to test functional relations and mechanisms, the ride's clearance envelope (the area within possible reach of the passengers in the vehicle), and potential collision components.

CAD software is an enormous improvement over methods that were employed as short as 30 years ago. The time required to create a roller coaster from scratch would be quite lengthy without using a computer because of the enormous number of calculations required. With a computer, changes and iterations can be made very rapidly. Multiple track variations for a ride may be presented to customers, enabling them to choose their favorite layouts. Then, when the CAD work is complete, the production data is electronically sent to the manufacturer or fabricator.

Modern day roller coasters are very precisely designed. Long gone are the days of trial and error. From paper and pencil to bending coat hangers to realistic 3D modeling, the methods for designing the ultimate scream machine have evolved enormously. The end result, however, remains the same.

The groundbreaking scream machines that shaped the evolution of the roller coaster made this list because they were the first of their kind, crossed a threshold that had never been broken before, or have some other historical or cultural significance. A clarification before we get to the list: Russian ice slides are the forefather of the roller coaster, but are not technically roller coasters, which is why I decided not to place them at #1 on this list, and instead mention them prior to the list. None of the roller coasters listed in this book would be here today if it had not been for the ice slides.

50 Groundbreaking Roller Coasters is based upon the opinions of the author and is not grounded in any scientific research. This book uses coaster and theme park terminology that I try to explain as we go along, but I've also included a glossary at the end of the book. Coasters are ranked in reverse order, 50 to 1, with 1 being, in my opinion, the most important. There are over 3,000 roller coasters currently operating worldwide today, and thousands of others that no longer exist, so narrowing a list to just 50 is quite daunting. Every ride description includes pertinent information and stats such as name, location, height, inversions, etc., as well as an explanation for why it made this list.

*Spoiler Alert: One of the most terrifying aspects of any thrill ride is the element of surprise. If you continue reading, the thrill of the attractions may be spoiled for you, as each ride listed contains a description of the elements that make it innovative or historic.

Now, on to the countdown...

The 50 Most Important Roller Coasters Ever Built

50. THE SMILER

Known for: World record holder for most inversions
Park: Alton Towers
Location: United Kingdom
Type: Steel
Opened: 2013
Designer/Manufacturer: John Wardley/Gerstlauer
Height (ft): 72
Drop (ft): 98
Speed (mph): 52.8
Inversions: 14
Video: https://www.youtube.com/watch?v=qqN9PDS3hOc

Picture every type of inversion you've ever seen or experienced on a roller coaster. Now combine them all on one ride, and you've got The Smiler at Alton Towers. The world record holder for most inversions on a roller coaster (with 14!), The Smiler seems to flip riders upside down every way imaginable: barrels rolls, cobra rolls, inverted drops, corkscrews, heartline rolls, dive loops, roll overs, and sidewinders. The 3,838 feet of track are crammed into a small area, with all of the inversions twisting around and through each other in a labyrinth of steel. There are two lift hills, the second of which gives riders a brief reprieve from all the insanity. Making matters more interesting is Alton Tower's restrictions regarding building tall rides above the height of the trees, resulting in the coaster being sunk down below grade. The Smiler has four more inversions than the next loopiest coaster, and pushes the limits of riders' endurance.

49. RAVEN

Known for: Template for small parks to follow
Park: Holiday World
Location: United States
Type: Wood
Opened: 1995
Designer/Manufacturer: Dennis McNulty, Larry Bill/Custom Coasters International
Height (ft): 80
Drop (ft): 85
Speed (mph): 48
Video: https://www.youtube.com/watch?v=fsiP6x9K_kk

Holiday World is set to launch America's first launched wing coaster, Thunderbird, in 2015. The theme park in Santa Claus, Indiana, has become a favorite of coaster enthusiasts, having been visited by over a million guests each of the last four years and featured on numerous Travel Channel programs. But it wasn't always this way.

Holiday World was virtually unknown and unheard of until the 1994 season, when they opened a small wooden roller coaster called Raven. And then everything changed. The Raven, which takes its name from Edgar Allan Poe's poem "The Raven," is a terrain coaster where the biggest drop occurs in the middle of the ride. The Raven borrowed elements from other famous coasters, and from 2000 to 2003 was voted the world's "Best Wooden Roller Coaster" at the Golden Ticket Awards, which are presented annually by *Amusement Today* magazine. Coaster fans flocked from all over the world to ride the award-winning Raven, which directly led to Holiday World's success and growth. The park's success was so great that other parks used it as a template—build a small, affordable, but wildly thrilling wooden coaster and enthusiasts will travel far distances to ride it. Quassy, Mount Olympus, Alabama Adventure, and ZDTs are amusement parks that built small but thrilling wooden coasters inspired by The Raven.

48. VILD-SVINET

Known for: First Eurofighter model
Park: BonBon-Land
Location: Denmark
Type: Steel
Opened: 2003
Designer/Manufacturer: Werner Stengel/Gerstlauer
Height (ft): 72
Speed (mph): 45
Inversions: 1
Video: https://www.youtube.com/watch?v=t4ICAJKD9rQ

Vild-Svinet (Danish for "The Wild Boar") is a steel roller coaster at BonBon-Land in southern Zealand, Denmark, approximately 62 miles (100 kilometers) from Copenhagen. Vild-Svinet is the prototype for the Gerstlauer Eurofighter roller coaster model. At 97 degrees, the coaster is the steepest in Denmark. 18 Eurofighter models have since been built, making up nearly a third of Gerstlauer's total coaster count.

47. FLYING TURNS

Known for: Modern wooden bobsled
Park: Knoebels
Location: United States
Type: Wood
Opened: 2013
Designer/Manufacturer: John Fetterman, from a 1920s design by John Miller and John Norman Bartlett/Knoebels Amusement Resort
Height (ft): 50
Speed (mph): 24
Video: https://www.youtube.com/watch?v=ZfgkNeXRDdY

Visitors to amusement parks throughout the 1930s and '40s were terrorized by a unique style of coaster—the flying turns. The flying turns style ride is essentially like a bobsled found in the Winter Olympics, only it runs on wheels and wood instead of blades and ice. The trains were free to roll around the trough so that subsequent rides may not take the exact same path through the course. The Lake Placid Bobsled built for Palisades Park, New Jersey, in 1937, was considered the fiercest flying turns style coaster. As with most of the turns, it only lasted a mere nine years before it was dismantled in 1946 due to low ridership, rider complaints, and mounting maintenance costs. The wooden bobsled eventually fell out of favor, the last closing in 1974, and modern bobsleds were built out of more durable steel and fiberglass.

That is until a little park in Pennsylvania decided to attempt the impossible—resurrect the wooden bobsled coaster and make it safe and efficient enough for modern standards. This daunting challenge almost proved to be too much. This engineering nightmare was scheduled to open in 2006, but the park soon discovered it would be harder than originally thought to get the trains to perform as expected. Multiple iterations of the vehicles were tested and modifications were made to the track without success. But the park persisted, kept iterating, brought in the best coaster designers, and, after seven years of work, The Flying Turns opened to the public in October 2013. The result of this labor of love is a 47-foot-tall, 1,200-foot-long ride with three lift hills, a 540-degree helix and a double figure-eight course, the bulk of which is constructed of southern yellow pine. Trains consist of three two-person cars that swoop and swerve as they negotiate the twists and turns. Flying Turns is also one of the rare coasters to contain three lift hills.

Flying Turns is a true hidden gem, and Knoebels is probably the only park in the world that could spend seven years developing a ride like this in full view of the public. Thank goodness they accomplished this incredible feat and the ride is open for us all to enjoy.

46. OBLIVION

Known for: World's first vertical drop roller coaster
Park: Alton Towers
Location: United Kingdom
Type: Steel
Opened: 1998
Designer/Manufacturer: John Wardley/Bolliger & Mabillard
Height (ft): 65
Drop (ft): 180
Speed (mph): 68.4
Video: https://www.youtube.com/watch?v=zcTDD0JR0SA

Oblivion is a steel roller coaster located at Alton Towers in England. The ride opened as the world's first vertical drop roller coaster on March 14, 1998, amidst a large publicity campaign. With a maximum speed of 68 mph, it is the third fastest roller coaster in the UK, behind Stealth at Thorpe Park and the Pepsi Max Big One at Blackpool

Pleasure Beach. It was also the first B&M dive coaster built.

The main feature of the dive coaster's is a dramatic pause at the top of the nearly vertical drop. Oblivion's cars were twice as wide as any other roller coaster vehicle at the time, sitting eight passengers across and affording more a front row seat and a clear view of straight-down ascent into a tiny, black hole. Today, dive coasters sit six, eight, or even ten passengers across. There's even an option to use floorless trains, meaning there's nothing but airtime between rider's dangling feet and the steel rails rushing by, adding another level of thrill. But it all started in the northern United Kingdom with Oblivion.

45. NEW TEXAS GIANT

Known for: Template for converting wood to steel coasters
Park: Six Flags Over Texas
Location: United States
Type: Steel
Opened: 2011
Designer/Manufacturer: Alan Schilke/Rocky Mountain Construction
Height (ft): 153
Drop (ft): 147
Speed (mph): 65
Video: https://www.youtube.com/watch?v=VtbCi6xts7s

Everything's bigger in Texas. When it opened in 1990, Texas Giant was the tallest wooden roller coaster in the world. In *Amusement Today's* Golden Ticket Awards, Texas Giant ranked as the number one wooden roller coaster for 1998 and 1999. Its ranking slowly declined to position 32 in 2009, its final year of operation as a wooden roller coaster. What do you do with a declining roller coaster that is showing its age? With mounting repair and maintenance costs, Six Flags decided to reinvigorate the classic coaster.

In 2009, Texas Giant closed to make way for the New Texas Giant, the first roller coaster to make use of the Rocky Mountain Construction I-Box Track. This new innovative track replaced the prior wooden track with steel beams, while the majority of the wooden support structure remained. The result: a butter smooth ride that offered a new, more intense experience while maintaining the look of a classic wooden roller coaster. Six Flags immediately had a huge hit on their hands.

Following its 2010 renovation, the New Texas Giant again

ranked highly in the Golden Ticket Awards (this time amongst steel roller coasters), achieving ranks of 6 and 5 in 2011 and 2012 respectively. The ride also won a Golden Ticket Award for being the Best New Ride of 2011, and instantly climbed to the top of enthusiasts' top 10 lists.

44. MEDUSA

Known for: First floorless coaster
Park: Six Flags Great Adventure
Location: United States
Type: Steel
Opened: 1999
Designer/Manufacturer: Werner Stengel/Bolliger & Mabillard
Height (ft): 142
Drop (ft): 132
Speed (mph): 61
Inversions: 7
Video: https://www.youtube.com/watch?v=Sbm5LcuPFkw

A variation on the standard sit-down roller coaster vehicle was introduced in 1999 at Six Flags Great Adventure. B&M began development between 1995 and 1996 before finally unveiling Medusa, the world's first floorless roller coaster. The vehicle sits above the track but contains no floor between the rider's feet and the rails, allowing their legs to dangle freely over the steel rails. It's like taking an inverted coaster car and putting it on a sit-down coaster's track. Because the vehicles have no floors, this design requires the station to have a retractable floor built in that can move into place after a train has parked to allow guests to safely board and disembark. When a fully loaded train is ready for dispatch, the floor disengages and folds up out of the way, allowing the train to pass.

The floorless coaster was a success. Four more B&M floorless roller coasters opened the year after Medusa. B&M also began offering floorless trains on their dive coaster models. For the 2015 season, Cedar Point converted their stand-up coaster, Mantis, into a floorless coaster, now called Rougarou. Once Rougarou opens, there will be 14 floorless coasters in operation worldwide (not including the dive coasters).

B&M is currently the only roller coaster manufacturer to have built a floorless model. Maurer Sohne have developed their own floorless vehicles, but to date have not sold any. Intamin's

SkyRush at HersheyPark features four-across seating, with the middle two seats having floors but the outer two do not.

In 2008, Medusa received a new paint job to go along with its new name and theme: Bizarro.

43. SANTA CRUZ GIANT DIPPER

Known for: One of the most-ridden coasters ever
Park: Santa Cruz Beach Boardwalk
Location: United States
Type: Wood
Opened: 1924
Designer/Manufacturer: Frank Prior, Frederick Church/Arthur Looff
Height (ft): 70
Drop (ft): 65
Speed (mph): 55
Video: https://www.youtube.com/watch?v=iV3hXbUJOAM

The Giant Dipper is a historic wooden roller coaster located at the Santa Cruz Beach Boardwalk, an amusement park in Santa Cruz, California. It took 47 days to build at a cost of $50,000, and opened on May 17, 1924. The beginning of the ride is unlike any other: the train dips into a black tunnel, twisting back and forth before hitting the 70-foot-tall lift hill. After that, it's just a beautifully paced ride in a beautiful setting. You'll be able to catch fleeting views of the beach while cresting the hills, before going out and back and out again. The back half of the ride is mostly hidden underneath the wooden structure and bounces beneath the rest of the track. 90-year-old roller coasters aren't supposed to go 55 mph, are they?

The Giant Dipper has received several awards, including a Golden Age Coaster award, a Coaster Landmark award, and being named a National Historic Landmark. It's also one of the most ridden roller coasters ever. As of 2012, over 60 million thrill seekers had gone for a ride. Are you one of them? If not, you should get to California as soon as you can.

42. HYPERSONIC XLC

Known for: First compressed air-launched coaster
Park: Kings Dominion
Location: United States
Type: Steel
Opened: 2001
Closed: 2007
Designer/Manufacturer: S&S Worldwide
Height (ft): 165
Drop (ft): 133
Speed (mph): 80
Video: https://www.youtube.com/watch?v=k3sjcnJlrts

Hypersonic XLC was the world's first compressed air-launched coaster. It was built by S&S Worldwide, a company specializing in air-powered rides such as Skyhawk and Power Tower at Cedar Point. Hypersonic was actually S&S Worldwide's prototype for an air-launched coaster, a model they called Thrust Air 2000.

The launch system for this eXtreme Launch Coaster (XLC) is similar to the hydraulic launch found on Intamin's accelerator coasters, in that a cable pulls a catch car that connects underneath of the train. The major difference is that the cable is powered by compressed air instead of nitrogen gas or oil. Acceleration is nearly constant, but the resulting loud noises caused by the whooshing air can be an annoying issue for theme parks. Pneumatic systems are technically simpler than hydraulics, but are also less powerful.

Hypersonic was capable of launching passengers from 0 to 80 mph in 1.8 seconds, and was considered to be the most intense launched coaster up to that point. But the launch turned out to be too intense and troublesome. In 2007, Hypersonic XLC was closed and later dismantled. The platform is all that remains at the ride's former location between the Hurler and Grizzly roller coasters.

41. KING COBRA

Known for: First stand-up coaster
Park: Kings Island
Location: United States
Type: Steel
Opened: 1984
Closed: 2001
Designer/Manufacturer: TOGO
Height (ft): 95
Speed (mph): 50
Inversions: 1

https://www.youtube.com/watch?v=Ta1flunrRPM

Two roller coasters in Japan were converted from sit-down to stand-up coasters, but the first roller coaster specifically designed to use stand-up trains from the beginning was King Cobra at Kings Island. After a right-hand turn off the 95-foot-high lift, the track drops down and into the coaster's single inversion, a tight vertical loop. Next, a rise into a hill leads into a downward spiraling helix. The track then makes a victory lap around the entire circuit with a few random bunny hops thrown in. Incidentally, the 24-passenger trains were not the most comfortable or male-friendly vehicles ever built.

After years of declining ridership and rising maintenance fees, King Cobra was dismantled and removed from the park in 2001. The stand-up coaster was a short-lived fad, with less than 30 being built worldwide between 1984 and 1998. A clone of King Cobra was built at Canada's Wonderland when Skyrider opened in 1985, but was closed forever in 2014.

40. KOBRA

Known for: First launch coaster
Park: Kings Dominion
Location: United States
Type: Steel
Opened: 1977
Closed: 1986
Designer/Manufacturer: Schwarzkopf
Height (ft): 137.8
Speed (mph): 53
Inversions: 1
Video: https://www.youtube.com/watch?v=MZDVTg-kcJs

In 1977, Kings Dominion's fourth roller coaster was one of the first rides to use a launch system rather than the typical chain lift to get up to its maximum potential energy. The King Kobra featured a 50-ton counterweight drop launch and was the park's first launched roller coaster. This system involved a catch car attaching itself to the train, which was attached to the weight via a cable. When the launch was triggered, the counterweight weight was dropped down a shaft, pulling the cable and catch car, which in turn pushed the train down the launch track.

King Kobra operated for nine seasons before being relocated to Jolly Roger Amusement Park in Ocean City, Maryland, and later to Hopi Hari in Brazil, where it exists today as Katapul. Kings Dominion would later make launch coaster history once again by opening just the second ride to utilize linear induction motors (Flight of Fear).

39. STEEL DRAGON 2000

Known for: World's longest roller coaster
Park: Nagashima Spa Land
Location: Japan
Type: Steel
Opened: 2000
Designer/Manufacturer: Steve Okamoto/Morgan Manufacturing
Height (ft): 318
Speed (mph): 95
Video: https://www.youtube.com/watch?v=klzlNeOmlJ8

Built by Morgan Manufacturing, this coaster opened, appropriately, in 2000—"The Year of the Dragon" in Asia. It debuted three months after Millennium Force at Cedar Point, and surpassed the former as the world's tallest complete-circuit coaster. It then lost its height record in 2003 when Cedar Point re-took the title with Top Thrill Dragster. But Steel Dragon 2000 also took the record for the longest track length—8,133 ft—which it still holds today. The ride is the second fastest coaster in Japan (behind Dodonpa) and the sixth fastest in the world.

To this day, Steel Dragon 2000 still reigns as the world's tallest non-launched roller coaster. Impressively, it is also the only coaster in the world to break the 8,000-foot length threshold. Four minutes may not seem like much, but it can be a loooooong time on a coaster—particularly one that rises a staggering 318 feet and reaches a mind-numbing speed of 95 mph. Steel Dragon 2000 was such an impressive accomplishment that, for only the second time in the company's history, Bolliger & Mabillard provided trains for a coaster they didn't build. The coaster did not operate from 2003 to 2006 due to a sheered axle that caused one of the original trains' cars to lose a wheel. It reopened sporting two new, sleek B&M trains carrying 28 riders sitting two abreast. Earthquake protection was a huge concern, so the structure uses far more steel then similar rides, which is why the cost ballooned to over $50 million dollars (compared with Millennium Force, which was just a cool $25 million).

38. SANTA MONICA WEST COASTER

Known for: Iconic steel roller coaster
Park: Pacific Park
Location: United States
Type: Steel
Opened: 1996
Designer/Manufacturer: Morgan Manufacturing
Height (ft): 55
Drop (ft): 20
Speed (mph): 35
Video: https://www.youtube.com/watch?v=bQI-_IFUDDU

West Coaster at Pacific Park is a family steel roller coaster that rises to a height of 55 feet and races at speeds of up to 35 mph along the world famous Santa Monica Pier. West Coaster begins with a helix, followed by a gentle first drop and a quick bunny hop, then concludes with one final helix before returning to the station.

If you've ever seen a roller coaster on TV, in a commercial, or in a movie, there's a good chance that it was Santa Monica Pier's. The coaster's proximity to several movie and television studios makes it a very accessible and popular location to shoot video. While the layout itself is rather uninspiring, it's location over the Pacific Ocean more than makes up for it. The West Coaster has no doubt inspired many to become lifelong roller coaster fans.

37. FORMULA ROSSA

Known for: World's fastest roller coaster
Park: Ferrari World Abu Dhabi
Location: Abu Dhabi, UAE
Type: Steel
Opened: 2010
Designer/Manufacturer: Sherif Bacheet/Intamin
Height (ft): 171
Drop (ft): 169
Speed (mph): 149
Video: https://www.youtube.com/watch?v=khRTNdEgZqg

You want velocity? Try this on for size: Formula Rossa's coaster train accelerates to its top speed in approximately five seconds using a hydraulic launch system that generates a release velocity similar to that of aircraft carrier steam catapults. By the way, that top speed is 240km/h (150 mph). The initial acceleration from standstill reaches 100km/h in two seconds, beating the best commercially available supercar (as of 2014) while allowing riders to experience 1.7G of force.

Formula Rossa is a hydraulic launched roller coaster located at Ferrari World in Abu Dhabi, United Arab Emirates. Manufactured by Intamin, this is easily the world's fastest roller coaster. High speeds combined with the risk of impacting airborne particulate such as sand or insects results in riders having to wear protective glasses similar to those used during skydiving. The layout is mostly comprised of a large figure-eight with low-to-the-ground turns and a series of bunny hops back towards the station. While the typical launched coaster shoots right into a large, oftentimes vertical hill, Formula Rossa launches into a more drawn-out hill, which is why it's also not the tallest roller coaster.

36. REVERE BEACH CYCLONE
Known for: First coaster to exceed 100 feet
Park: Revere Beach
Location: United States
Type: Wood
Opened: 1925
Closed: 1969
Designer/Manufacturer: Fredrick Church/Traver Engineering
Height (ft): 100
Speed (mph): 45
Video: https://www.youtube.com/watch?v=I5cJDnbk7cg

     If a new roller coaster is built today and is less than 100 feet tall, it's considered to be "small," or might be classified as a "family coaster." Until 1925, no roller coaster had ever crossed the 100-foot threshold—that is until the creators of the Cyclone dared to. When the Cyclone opened at Revere Beach in 1925 it was the tallest roller coaster ever built up to that point. Not to be confused with the Lightning roller coaster, one of Harry Traver's "terrible trio," the 3,600-foot-long wooden Cyclone was assembled at a cost of just $125,000, and had a top speed of around 45 miles per hour. Cyclone held the title of world's tallest roller coaster until 1964, when it was surpassed by Montaña Rusa at La Feria Chapultepec Mágico in Mexico City, Mexico. Not long after, Cyclone was shuttered in 1969. The structure remained for another five years, even surviving a fire in 1971 before finally being torn down for good in 1974.

35. MONTEZUM

Known for: South America's only operating wood coaster
Park: Hopi Hari
Location: Brazil
Type: Wood
Opened: 1999
Designer/Manufacturer: Roller Coaster Corporation of America
Height (ft): 138
Drop (ft): 144
Speed (mph): 64
Video: https://www.youtube.com/watch?v=oz7PTf-nynA

Montezum is the only operating wooden roller coaster in South America, and the only one built in the modern era. The 64 mph ride dominates the skyline of Hopi Hari theme park in São Paulo, Brazil. The twisted layout includes a tunnel under the entrance road to the park and makes use of the hilly terrain to keep the thrills going all the way to the end. Assembled over a span of eighteen months, more than 1,500 workers helped construct the massive wooden structure. Montezum wasn't the first wooden coaster built in South America, as one called Montaña Rusa was designed by the famous Harry Traver, and operated from 1938 to 1947. South Americans had to wait 52 to years to finally ride a classic, wooden roller coaster but it was worth the wait.

34. X2

Known for: First 4th dimension coaster
Park: Six Flags Magic Mountain
Location: United States
Type: Steel
Opened: 2002
Designer/Manufacturer: Alan Schilke, Renato Manzoni/Arrow Dynamics
Height (ft): 190
Drop (ft): 215
Speed (mph): 76
Inversions: 2
Video: https://www.youtube.com/watch?v=8WTD0Hc9anw

There's nothing ordinary about X2 at Six Flags Magic Mountain. The seats are cantilevered to either side of the track, just like a wing coaster, but with an extra twist—they can rotate 360 degrees. It's like a spin-and-puke carnival ride and a hyper coaster had a lovechild together. The demented designers at Arrow drew up this wicked machine that was later perfected by S&S Worldwide. The controlled spinning or rotation is in a direction that is independent of the track—hence the assertion that it is like a fourth dimension. There are two sets of rails—one supports the weight of the vehicles, while the other is what makes the seats rotate. The vertical distance or displacement between the two sets of rails controls the rotation of the passengers by transforming linear motion into rotational motion, accomplished via a rack and pinion gear.

Here's how it works: The pinion, a typical circular gear, engages the teeth on a linear gear bar (also known as a rack). Thus, as the spacing between the rails changes, the wheels connected to the rack move vertically up or down, causing the pinion gear (or gears) to rotate, flipping the seats as much as 720 degrees. Pushing the rack up causes the seats to spin in one direction, whereas pulling the rack down causes the seats to flip in the opposite direction. The amount of rotation is proportional to the displacement between the two sets of rails. No separate power supply is required; the forward motion of the vehicle due to gravity is enough. The pinion gear may actually use a complete gearbox in order to achieve the perfect ratio of linear to rotational motion. Of course, it's not as simple as it sounds because there has to be flexibility built into the system due to vibrations and imperfections in the manufacture of the rails.

With its 360-degree rotating seats and headfirst, face-down drops, X2 is easily one of the most intense thrill rides on the planet. Riders depart the station facing backwards, so the long climb up the hill is quite agonizing. Let's just get this over with! Before long the top of the hill is reached, and then after a small dip the seats rotate forward, bringing you around to face the ground 200 feet below you. You drop straight down, face first, before rotating onto your back midway through the drop, the heavy g-forces pushing you into the seat. After the first drop, the train enters an inside raven loop. As it exits the loop, the seats rotate, executing a lie-to-fly maneuver, which transitions the riders from lying on their backs above the track facing backwards to a flying position hanging under the track facing forward. Shortly after exiting the first vertical turn, and while still in the flying position, the seats do a 360-degree rotation backwards, completing a full backflip. Just when you think you can't take anymore, X2 negotiates its most demented inversion—the half-half, a unique half-twist/forward flip where the track does a 180 roll while the seats perform half a rotation. Then another raven turn leads into a fly-to-lie maneuver that transitions the train back on top of the track and the riders onto their backs, looking backward again. Just as soon as you get your bearings, giant flamethrowers spit fire overhead, leaving you in awe.

No matter how many coaster notches you have on your belt, you've never experienced anything quite like X2—perhaps the most terrifying roller coaster you can ride today.

33. THE LOST COASTER

Known for: First wooden coaster to use magnetic brakes
Park: Indiana Beach
Location: United States
Type: Wood
Opened: 2002
Designer/Manufacturer: Custom Coasters International
Height (ft): 35
Speed (mph): 20
Video: https://www.youtube.com/watch?v=yqhRvARZ38Y

For the next coaster on the list, we visit the small lakeside park of Indiana Beach in Monticello, Indiana, home to one of the most unique wooden coasters ever built. The Lost Coaster of Superstition Mountain (possibly the longest name of any coaster in existence) began as a small mine-themed, powered dark ride, but in 2002 it was completely renovated by Custom Coasters Inc. (CCI) to become the compact coaster it is today. This was also the last project CCI fully completed before they went under later that year.

Lost Coaster uses custom-made two-car trains by CCI that can turn on a dime. The ride's curves may have the tightest radius of any roller coaster ever built. Each car holds up to four passengers that sit facing inwards. A vertical elevator lift takes the vehicles to the top of the "mountain" before depositing them into caverns full of surprising turns and sudden drops. The ride does feel like an out-of-control mine train, racing through sharp bends and oddly banked track as you're taken around, in, and out of the mountain.

Lost Coaster is also significant because it was the first wooden coaster to use magnetic brakes. This technology is better than the standard friction brakes because there is no physical contact between the vehicle and the brake fins, thus no wear and tear and less overall maintenance. It's not easy to get to, Indiana Beach being located in the middle of nowhere, but the trek is worth it to experience this quirky little ride.

32. KINGDA KA/TOP THRILL DRAGSTER

Kingda Ka Stats:

Known for: World's tallest free-standing coaster

Park: Six Flags Great Adventure

Location: United States

Type: Steel

Opened: 2005

Designer/Manufacturer: Werner Stengel/Intamin

Height (ft): 456

Drop (ft): 418

Speed (mph): 128

Video: https://www.youtube.com/watch?v=HN8nv4tVFuA

Top Thrill Dragster Stats:

Known for: First full-circuit roller coaster to exceed 400 feet

Park: Cedar Point

Location: United States

Type: Steel

Opened: 2003

Designer/Manufacturer: Werner Stengel/Intamin

Height (ft): 420

Drop (ft): 400

Speed (mph): 120

Video: https://www.youtube.com/watch?v=nAOQBlDDC7M

The number 32 coaster on our list is actually a tie between Kingda Ka and Top Thrill Dragster. These extremely similar rides opened within two years of each other, with Top Thrill Dragster being the first to breach the 400 foot plateau for a full-circuit coaster, and Kingda Ka breaking its height and speed records shortly thereafter. The major differences between the two are that Kingda Ka has a dual loading station (meaning it has two tracks side-by-side), Dragster has lap bar restraints while Ka's are over-the-shoulder, and Ka has an additional airtime hill leading into the brake run.

Kingda Ka at Six Flags Great Adventure in Jackson, New

Jersey, is the world's tallest free-standing roller coaster at 456 feet. This king of coasters is launched by a hydraulic motor to 128 miles per hour (206 km/h) in 3.5 seconds, making it the second fastest coaster in the world (we'll examine how a hydraulic launch system works in an upcoming coaster). At the end of the launch track, the train climbs the main top hat tower, reaching its maximum height before spiraling straight down. The train speeds into a second hill of 129 feet before smoothly slowing to a stop via magnetic brakes. The entire ride covers the 3,118-foot-long (950 m) track in less than a minute, but it's one that will stick with you forever.

31. RIVERVIEW BOBS

Known for: Famous wooden coaster
Park: Riverview Park (Chicago)
Location: United States
Type: Wood
Opened: 1924
Closed: 1967
Designer/Manufacturer: Fred Church/Frank Prior and Fredrick Church
Height (ft): 87
Drop (ft): 85
Speed (mph): 50
Video: https://www.youtube.com/watch?v=H0P6_FAS6TM

If you asked a roller coaster enthusiast what the ultimate roller coaster ever built was, their answer could be a surprising one: the Bobs at Riverview Park. Built in 1924, this aggressive coaster was only 87 feet tall, but the 85-foot drop and 50 mph speeds made this compact, diabolical coaster more ferocious than it looked. The density and proximity of the wooden trestles to the track made the cars feel like they were flying around faster than they truly were. Bobs had a very good capacity for a coaster—over 1,200 people per hour could brave the monster thanks to the three 11-car trains. At one point the Bobs was also listed in the Guinness Book of World Records, not for any notable record relating to the ride itself, but for the number of lost earrings.

Sadly, the Bobs was demolished with the rest of the park in 1967 so a shopping mall could be built in its place. The Raging Wolf Bobs at Geauga Lake was inspired by the original, but was said to be less intense. Unfortunately for coaster fans, even the sequel is no longer operating today.

30. FRED CHURCH'S TORNADO

Known for: Church's Haunted Coaster
Park: Coney Island
Location: United States
Type: Wood
Opened: 1926
Closed: 1978
Designer/Manufacturer: Frank Darling, Frank Prior, Fred Church, LaMarcus A. Thompson
Height (ft): 71
Video: https://www.youtube.com/watch?v=ZtxtOH3ywU4

Located just down the street from the infamous Coney Island Cyclone stood one of Fred Church's best designs: the Tornado. The twisted contortion of track was cramped into a narrow plot of land and wrapped itself around a large tower. Tornado was a hybrid coaster, consisting of a wooden track built on top of a steel structure much like the neighboring Cyclone. The ride began with a long dark tunnel before climbing the 71-foot-tall lift. What followed was a seemingly endless bowl of tight turns and sudden drops.

Tornado was built at a cost of $250,000 by the L.A. Thompson Company, and it was said that the company's founder could be seen working in the tower in the middle of the ride, despite the fact that LaMarcus Thompson had died years earlier. The coaster was often referred to as "Church's Haunted Coaster," but this distinction couldn't help save the ride. It was demolished in 1978 without much fanfare, as it had always been overshadowed by the famous Cyclone. Some say the Cyclone was the coaster that should have been bulldozed, and the Tornado maintained.

29. EL CONDOR

Known for: First Vekoma SLC
Park: Walibi Holland
Location: Netherlands
Type: Steel
Opened: 1994
Designer/Manufacturer: Vekoma
Height (ft): 102
Speed (mph): 50
Inversions: 5
Video: https://www.youtube.com/watch?v=vnerotGoH2s

There are over 3,000 roller coasters operating worldwide today, but what the average amusement park-goer may not realize is that many of them are "clones"—rides that are exactly the same as others in different parks. From the coaster manufacturers' perspective, this is a good business practice because it is cheaper to design one ride and sell it over and over again than it is to design an entirely new ride every single time. Vekoma could be considered the most successful roller coaster manufacturer ever, based on the number of cloned rides they've been able to sell. RCBD lists 50 installations of Vekoma's boomerang coasters and 41 suspended looping coaster (SLC) models.

Walibi Holland's El Condor was the very first suspended looping coaster to open. The 102-foot-tall inverted coaster began terrorizing the Netherlands in 1994. While many coaster enthusiasts are not fans of the SLCs, they are one of the most successful coaster models ever built. You won't have to travel far to find one near you. In fact, Vekoma probably would have built many more if their design wasn't being copied and sold by several Asian companies.

28. SKYTRAK

Known for: World's first "flying" coaster
Park: Granada Studios
Location: United Kingdom
Type: Steel
Opened: 1997
Closed: 1998
Designer/Manufacturer: Skytrak International
Height (ft): 50
Speed (mph): 28

"It's a bird! It's a plane! It's Superman!" That's what visitors to Granada Studios were exclaiming in 1997 as they witnessed other humans soaring over their heads. Contrary to popular belief, Skytrak was the world's first "flying" roller coaster—a type of coaster where passengers lie prone with their bodies parallel to the track. Designed and built by Skytrak International, a subsidiary of Fairpoint Engineering, nobody had ever seen or experienced anything like Skytrak before. To board the tortuous-looking vehicle was almost like climbing a ladder, very similar to the Volare flying coasters built by Zamperla today. The single rail track twisted above Granada Studios in several large turns, spiraling helixes, and small bunny hops.

The experience of flying solo was unique, but at a cost to the ride's throughput (THRC), with only one rider per car and only five cars operating at once (though it was rare for all five to run). The ride was plagued with mechanical issues, including a derailment during a test run. The £1 million investment closed in 1998, and immediately dismantled and scrapped. The park itself ran into financial problems and ended up closing the same year. The next flying coaster—and the first successful one—was Stealth at Paramount's Great America, designed by Vekoma (currently called Nighthawk, and located at Carowinds).

27. XCELERATOR

Known for: First hydraulically launched coaster
Park: Knott's Berry Farm
Location: United States
Type: Steel
Opened: 2002
Designer/Manufacturer: Werner Stengel/Intamin
Height (ft): 205
Drop (ft): 200
Speed (mph): 82
Video: https://www.youtube.com/watch?v=NJE7eOqo1B8

Xcelerator is a steel launched roller coaster at Knott's Berry Farm in Buena Park, California. The ride was the world's first roller coaster to utilize a hydraulic launch where a catch car, called a sled, connected to a cable that latches on to a mechanism attached to the underside of the coaster train. The catch car moves in its own track or "groove" in the center of the launch track. The hydraulic motor is located at one end of the launch track and the waiting train at the other. Think of it like a giant fishing pole that reels a train in super-fast before being released.

Here's how it works: Hydraulic fluid is pumped into several different hydraulic accumulators (energy storing devices), comprised of two compartments separated by a piston. As the incompressible hydraulic fluid is pumped into one compartment, a gas in the other compartment is compressed. The nitrogen in the accumulator tanks starts to go under pressure as hydraulic oil is pumped into the tanks. Once the nitrogen is compressed to an extremely high pressure, the pumping stops and the nitrogen goes into a cylinder block.

At launch, the fluid under pressure from the accumulators is used to drive either 16 or 32 hydraulic motors connected to an internal ring gear. The power from all of the motors is transferred to the giant cable drum by a planetary gearbox. The cable drum spins, rapidly winding the cable attached to the sled hooked under the train, accelerating it in a matter of seconds. The train is released from the sled and speeds through the rest of the course, but the sled and cable drum must decelerate rapidly and then return to their initial starting positions to launch the next train.

Typically, there are two sensors mounted to the top of the tallest hill immediately after the launch track. The distance between the two sensors is known so the control system can take that value and divide it by the time it takes the train to get from one sensor to the other. This gives the computer the train's speed going over the top of the hill. For every single launch, the information is recorded and plotted as a performance curve. The computer takes the average speed of the three previous trains and compares it to past launches in order to determine the power to give to the hydraulic motor. This way, if the first three trains are filled with swimsuit models and the fourth train is carrying football players, the power is enough to get the car over the hill.

Hydraulic launch systems are considered capable of giving a far greater and smoother acceleration than current electromagnetic propulsion style rides. The acceleration from a hydraulic system remains nearly constant throughout the entirety of the launch. However, the number of moving parts makes this system generally less reliable than magnetic systems, which contain no moving parts. Hydraulic launch systems have the highest power output and are compact, but the whole cable drive part is complicated due to the forces and speeds.

Xcelerator was basically a trial for the taller and faster Top Thrill Dragster at Cedar Point. Formula Rossa at Ferrari World in Abu Dhabi, United Arab Emirates, is currently the world's fastest roller coaster thanks to its hydraulic motor, achieving an amazing speed of 240 km/h (150 mph) in 4.9 seconds!

26. CYCLONE
Known for: World-famous coaster
Park: Coney Island
Location: United States
Type: Wood
Opened: 1927
Designer/Manufacturer: Vernon Keenan/Harry C. Baker
Height (ft): 85
Drop (ft): 85
Speed (mph): 60
Video: https://www.youtube.com/watch?v=lxSCNto21mU

Cyclone at Coney Island is arguably the most famous roller coaster in the world. Even if you've never had the pleasure of riding it before, you are no doubt aware of its existence. This wicked wooden twister with its iconic white structure is well known for its steep drops and notable airtime. Cyclone was among the first coasters to use steel trestlework in support of the wooden track. The original trains with fixed position lap bars and no seat dividers allowed riders to be tossed from side to side. The popularity of the tried and true design helped spawn countless copies and clones, including the Texas Cyclone at the defunct Six Flags Astroworld park.

After nearly 90 years, the Cyclone is still going strong, in part because of the tender love and care it has received over the years. Renowned modern wood coaster builder Great Coasters International was recently brought in to repair and rework the classic coaster to help keep the New York City landmark going strong for many years to come.

25. RYE AEROPLANE
Known for: Legendary "lost" coaster
Park: Rye Playland
Location: United States
Type: Wood
Opened: 1928
Closed: 1957
Designer/Manufacturer: Fredrick Church
Height (ft): 90
Speed (mph): 40
Video: https://www.youtube.com/watch?v=vkQlay9t76c

The Airplane (a.k.a. Aero Dips and Aeroplane) roller coaster is a lost classic. This masterpiece of thrills and aesthetics was designed by Fred Church. The all-wooden thrill ride opened along with the New York's Rye Beach Playland Park on May 26, 1928. The layout was known for its many tall spiraling drops, hills, bobs, and weaves, all set amidst disorienting layers of track. The cost of construction was under $200,000, and the coaster stood around 90 feet tall. According to Richard Munch's book *Harry G. Traver: Legends of Terror*, the track was somewhere between 3,135 and 3,560 feet in length. People who remember this coaster recall it as "looming" and "intimidating." Having built many ocean pier-based coasters in the early 1920s, Church was a master at condensing a compact layout in a small parcel of land. The Airplane's younger and tamer neighbor, the Dragon Coaster, had more of a widespread layout that took up about twice as much land.

The relatively unstable ground on which the Airplane was built, along with the intense pressure of the ride's forces, led to the coaster's high-maintenance reputation, and made repetitive riding difficult. When Westchester County changed insurance providers in 1957, inspectors of the ride said it would take about $100,000 to bring the Airplane up to current safety standards. That was too much for the county to want to spend on an amusement ride repair, so it was unceremoniously demolished in November of 1957. The Airplane is one of the top legendary roller coasters to no longer exist. If there were one roller coaster that could be rebuilt, a majority of coaster fanatics would choose the Rye Aeroplane.

24. CYCLONE RACER
Known for: Fredrick Church's only racing coaster
Park: The Pike, Long Beach, California
Location: United States
Type: Wood
Opened: 1930
Closed: 1968
Designer/Manufacturer: Harry G Traver
Height (ft): 65
Speed (mph): 50
Video: https://www.youtube.com/watch?v=Qp9gu2p9i_k

After Kings Island's Racer, the second most important racing coaster ever built, and maybe the most famous, was the Cyclone Racer. A racing roller coaster is comprised of two separate tracks, built side by side. Trains are often released at the same time so that they "race" each other. Cyclone Racer struck a majestic image, as the wooden structure protruded out into the Pacific Ocean. The total height of the coaster, including the pilings it stood on, was 110 feet.

Cyclone Racer's close proximity to Hollywood resulted in it appearing in many television shows, like *Leave It to Beaver*, and movies, such as the final car chase scene of the 1963 movie *It's a Mad Mad Mad Mad World*. Cyclone Racer, along with Rye Aeroplane and Crystal Beach Cyclone, is one of the top classic coasters fans hope will be rebuilt one day.

23. THE BEAST

Known for: Longest wood coaster
Park: Kings Island
Location: United States
Type: Wood
Opened: 1979
Designer/Manufacturer: Al Collins, Jeff Gramke, John C. Allen
Height (ft): 110
Drop (ft): 141
Speed (mph): 64.8
Video: https://www.youtube.com/watch?v=9dC6uJDNf64

The Beast opened on April 14, 1979, as the tallest, fastest, and longest wooden roller coaster in the world—and it has more than lived up to its name. This monstrosity is still the longest wooden roller coaster in the world, lasting more than four minutes and sprawling over 35 densely wooded acres on the outskirts of Kings Island. The Beast originally featured three underground tunnels. By its second season, the second and third underground tunnels had been enclosed into one long one so that an access road could be built. While legendary during the daytime, the Beast becomes an absolutely terrifying experience after nightfall. The number of tunnels suddenly becomes irrelevant as the darkness of the forest makes it impossible to determine when you're in a tunnel and when you're simply under the trees.

The Beast is often considered to be one of the best wooden

roller coasters in the world. In its lifetime it has given more than 45 million rides. The ride was so popular that it even spawned a sequel, Son of Beast, which we'll get to shortly. It's hard to imagine an amusement park ever building a ride as ambitious as The Beast, or one that sprawls over as much wooded countryside. It truly is one of a kind.

The legendary coaster obviously had a large impact on R.L Stine, a children's literature author from Columbus, Ohio, who wrote a book about a fictional version of the ride called *The Beast*, and a sequel called *The Beast 2*.

22. COLOSSUS

Known for: Moviestar coaster
Park: Six Flags Magic Mountain
Location: United States
Type: Wood
Opened: 1978
Closed: 2014
Designer/Manufacturer: International Amusement Devices
Height (ft): 125
Drop (ft): 115
Speed (mph): 62
Video: https://www.youtube.com/watch?v=tK4p7A_ReGk

In 1978, Colossus was the tallest and fastest roller coaster in the world. This mammoth wooden racing coaster was the first ride to contain two drops over 100 feet tall. Colossus became a very recognizable coaster after appearances in film and television, including the box office hit *National Lampoon's Vacation* and the opening title sequence of *Step by Step* from ABC's TGIFriday. After more than 36 years in operation, Six Flags announced that the roller coaster would be closed permanently on August 16, 2014, to become a single steel coaster called Twisted Colossus, another Rocky Mountain Construction transformation project like New Texas Giant.

21. THE BAT

Known for: World's first suspended coaster
Park: Kings Island
Location: United States
Type: Steel
Opened: 1981
Closed: 1983
Designer/Manufacturer: Arrow Dynamics
Height (ft): 78
Drop (ft): 70
Speed (mph): 51
Video: http://www.youtube.com/watch?v=Sg-OWKFyp8A

One of the most notorious rides in roller coaster history is The Bat at Kings Island. It was the first-ever suspended roller coaster, where the cars hang below the rails and are free to swing freely from side to side. The Bat only operated sporadically between 1981 and 1983 before being dismantled in 1985. Over the years, the legend of the Bat has grown due to the outrageous rumors about why the ride was destroyed, and because so few people were able to ride it. Contrary to many wild stories, the Bat never killed or even injured a rider. Poor engineering of the trains, track, and structure is what really led to the ride's demise. A year after the Bat was removed, the Vortex looping coaster was erected in its place, and actually reused the station. Concrete footers from the Bat can still be seen beneath the Vortex's structure. The suspended roller coaster returned to Kings Island in 1993 with the addition of Top Gun (renamed Flight Deck, and later themed to the Bat). If you were fortunate enough to ride the original Bat, consider yourself lucky!

20. OUTLAW RUN

Known for: First wooden roller coaster with multiple inversions
Park: Silver Dollar City
Location: United States
Type: Wood
Opened: 2013
Designer/Manufacturer: Alan Schilke/Rocky Mountain Construction
Height (ft): 107
Drop (ft): 162
Speed (mph): 68
Video: https://www.youtube.com/watch?v=-KqDI599wvE

Outlaw Run was the first wooden roller coaster manufactured by Rocky Mountain Construction, and the first built with multiple inversions, in which riders are turned upside-down and then back upright. The 2,937-foot-long (895 m) ride features three inversions and a top speed of 109 km/h (68 mph), making Outlaw Run the second-fastest wooden roller coaster in the world. The 162-foot-tall (49 m) first drop of the ride is the second steepest in the world, at 81° beyond horizontal.

Relative newcomers on the coaster design scene, Rocky Mountain Construction have developed a new wood coaster technology. "Topper track" replaces the top two pieces of a wood coaster's stack with steel and allows wooden coasters to do things they've never done before (and maybe were never meant to do). The first of these new hybrid wooden coasters opened in 2013 at Silver Dollar City.

Outlaw Run was the first looping wooden coaster since Son of Beast's loop was removed in 2006. The train plunges through three elements that have never been seen on a wooden coaster before—a 153° inverting over-banked turn, a double barrel roll, and a wave turn that provides unique, lateral airtime.

19. BOOMERANG
Known for: First boomerang coaster to open to public
Park: Bellewaerde Park
Location: Belgium
Type: Steel
Opened: 1984
Designer/Manufacturer: Vekoma
Height (ft): 116
Speed (mph): 46
Inversions: 3
Video: https://www.youtube.com/watch?v=NJLCv6cCgoc

If Vekoma's suspended looping coaster (SLC) is the second most popular roller coaster to be cloned, then the most popular and successful model is the boomerang, with over 50 installations worldwide. This type of coaster is referred to as a "shuttle coaster" because the track is not a complete circuit. The trains proceed up the initial lift backwards until they reach the apex, where they are released and roll forward through three inversions. The trains climb another lift hill before being released backwards through the same course, meaning riders are inverted upside-down a total of six times.

Belgium's Bellewaerde was just the second park to build a Vekoma boomerang coaster. However, Bellewaerde gets to call theirs a world first because the first boomerang that was built in Mexico had technical issues that delayed the opening of the ride. Thus, Bellewaerde had the first working boomerang coaster ever.

18. RUNAWAY MINE TRAIN

Known for: First Arrow mine train
Park: Six Flags Over Texas
Location: United States
Type: Steel
Opened: 1966
Designer/Manufacturer: Arrow Dynamics
Height (ft): 35
Speed (mph): 35
Video: https://www.youtube.com/watch?v=uHPbD8WqRC0

Arrow Dynamics helped Walt Disney achieve his dream of riding a bobsled down the Matterhorn mountain by employing the first use of tubular steel rails. They followed up that major success with the Runaway Mine Train at Six Flags Over Texas. The coaster made up for its small height by having three lift hills and two tunnels, including the world's first underwater coaster tunnel.

The classic ride was the first of many mine train roller coasters built across the United States. Almost every steel roller coaster between 1966 and 2011 used tubular steel rails (Rocky Mountain Construction now uses I-box shaped track beginning, with New Texas Giant in 2011). The Arrow Development Company, with Ronald Toomer, Karl Bacon, and Ed Morgan, advanced the steel roller coaster and roller coaster technology in general into a new, high-tech era.

17. SUPERMAN: THE ESCAPE

Known for: First coaster to top 100 miles per hour
Park: Six Flags Magic Mountain
Location: United States
Type: Steel
Opened: 1997
Designer/Manufacturer: Intamin
Height (ft): 415
Drop (ft): 328
Speed (mph): 100
Video: https://www.youtube.com/watch?v=JAYjWKAvysc

A roller coaster reaching speeds of 100 mph? It was unthinkable until Superman: The Escape opened in 1997. With the use of linear synchronous motors (LSMs) the car is accelerated from zero to 100 mph in seven heart-pounding seconds. LSMs use the basic magnetism theories of attraction and repulsion. Strong, permanent, rare-earth (those which come out of the ground magnetized) magnets are attached to the train. As with LIMs, electromagnets are secured to the track. When the train approaches one of the track-magnets, the track-magnet is set to attract the magnets on the train, pulling it forward. After the train passes over the track-magnet, the track-magnet is reversed to repel the train magnet, pushing the train down the track. Multiple sets of electromagnets on the track must be fired in sequence, switching polarity very quickly by the use of computers and electricity, in order to propel the train to top speed. Riders experience several blissful seconds of airtime before falling back to Earth and returning down the same track they were launched from (the track is not a complete circuit, and looks like a giant L).

For the 2011 season, Superman: The Escape was transformed into Superman: Escape from Krypton. The most significant change was turning the vehicles around to face the opposite direction, so passengers are launched backwards initially rather than forwards, and now look towards the ground rather than the sky on the vertical tower track.

16. FIREBALL
Known for: First modern wood coaster in China
Park: Happy Valley
Location: China
Type: Wood
Opened: 2009
Designer/Manufacturer: The Gravity Group
Height (ft): 108
Drop (ft): 103
Speed (mph): 56
Video: https://www.youtube.com/watch?v=0a9DPi1pGOE

There's been an explosion of amusement parks in China thanks to the rapidly expanding middle class. People with more disposable income can afford to spend on leisure activities like theme park visits. But there was a lack of large theme parks until very recently, and the expansion boom is still continuing. Some absolutely incredible theme parks are being built, and with them some crazy new roller coasters.

Happy Valley's Fireball is China's first modern wooden roller coaster. Since it opened in 2009, 10 more wooden coasters have opened or are under construction, and virtually all of them have been designed by American companies Great Coasters International or The Gravity Group. Sitting in a country like American, where wooden coasters have been present for more than a hundred years, it's hard to believe that a country as large as China has only had a wooden coaster for a few years.

15. SON OF BEAST

Known for: Biggest wooden coaster ever built
Park: Kings Island
Location: United States
Type: Wood
Opened: 2000
Closed: 2009
Designer/Manufacturer: Werner Stengel/Roller Coaster Corporation of America
Height (ft): 218
Drop (ft): 214
Speed (mph): 78.4
Video: https://www.youtube.com/watch?v=8GPmlW629e4

Anytime a Hollywood movie is successful, a sequel is made—and the same can now be said of roller coasters. Based on the success and popularity of The Beast, Kings Island decided to make a "sequel" ride, dubbed Son of Beast. The son would outdo the father in many ways. It was the tallest and fastest wooden roller coaster ever built, and the first wooden hyper coaster (a coaster over 200 feet tall). Son of Beast smashed nearly every wooden coaster record, except that it was designed just short enough so that The Beast retained its longest wooden roller coaster record. Opened on May 26, 2000 at Kings Island in Mason, Ohio, Son of Beast boasted a 214-foot (65 m) drop and a terrifying 118-foot-tall vertical loop. Although the supports for the loop were formed from steel, Son of Beast was technically the first modern looping wooden coaster in the world. It also once held the record for longest roller coaster with a loop, an honor now owned by California Screamin' at Disney California Adventure.

After numerous problems and an accident, the vertical loop was removed at the end of the 2006 season for maintenance reasons. Following another incident, Son of Beast closed permanently in 2009 and was left standing but not operating (SBNO) for many years (and $30+ million down the drain). Ironically, the out-of-commission ride was located in the Action Zone section of the park. Finally, in July 2012, it was announced that the ride would be dismantled and removed. The Banshee inverted coaster now resides on the hillside once dominated by Son of Beast and has a nice "eternal flame" tribute to the former mega coaster.

14. BATMAN THE RIDE
Known for: World's first inverted roller coaster
Park: Six Flags Great America
Location: United States
Type: Steel
Opened: 1992
Designer/Manufacturer: Werner Stengel/ Bolliger & Mabillard
Height (ft): 105
Drop (ft): 84.5
Speed (mph): 50
Video: https://www.youtube.com/watch?v=g_zJGTO_DvQ

For over a hundred years, roller coasters had the same basic configuration, with the seats sitting above the rails. That is until B&M had the novel idea of hanging the seats below the rails, like a chair lift at a ski resort. Six Flags Great America decided to take on the risk of building one of these never-before-seen rides, and it paid off big time. Batman: The Ride was the first inverted roller coaster ever built, and was awarded landmark status by the American Coaster Enthusiasts (ACE). The ride was so successful it spawned a dozen clones at amusement parks around the world. Successive inverted coasters were progressively taller and faster, but none may match the intensity and excitement per foot of the original.

After operating the same way for over 20 years, Six Flags wanted to do something special and unique. One of their evil geniuses had the brilliant idea to run the ride backwards for a limited time. A special chassis had to be designed and built in order for this to work. What was already an intense experience was instantly magnified. Just going up the lift backwards, not being able to see the top and having to stare at the ground, increased the scariness factor. Coaster enthusiasts affectionately labeled this version of the ride "Namtab" (Batman spelled backwards).

13. FLIGHT OF FEAR

Known for: World's first roller coaster to feature an LIM launch
Park: Kings Island
Location: United States
Type: Steel
Opened: 1996
Designer/Manufacturer: Werner Stengel/Premier Rides
Height (ft): 74.2
Speed (mph): 54
Inversions: 4
Video: https://www.youtube.com/watch?v=z32Kw698ybw

In 1996, The Outer Limits: Flight of Fear at Kings Island became the first roller coaster to use electromagnetic propulsion to launch the trains to their maximum kinetic energy (rather than using the traditional chain lift). Flight of Fear was manufactured by Premier Rides, and its highest point is 74 feet tall. All 2,705 feet of track are enclosed in a large warehouse-type building. Earthlings enter the attraction through a large alien spaceship. The electromagnetic launch takes three megawatts of power to accelerate the trains from zero to 60 mph in less than four seconds. Abductees are flown threw four inversions, but it may seem like many more than that when you're flying around in total darkness.

How does it work? Linear induction motors use multiple sets of high powered electromagnets secured to the track, and a gap is left in between each set. Alternating current (AC) is applied to the magnets to create a magnetic field. A metal fin attached to the bottom of the train passes through the gap between the magnets while the magnetic field creates a wave for the fin to ride and propels the train forward down the track.

Flight of Fear paved the way for many taller and faster launched rides that now hold the records for tallest and fastest roller coasters. The launch had a quick and powerful acceleration, meaning a large roller coaster could be fit into a small footprint, since a large, space-eating lift hill was no longer required. The Outer Limits portion of the name was dropped before the start of the

2001 season when the licensing agreement expired. The restraints were also changed in 2001, from over-the-shoulder harnesses to individual lap bars.

12. KUMBA

Known for: First B&M sit-down looper
Park: Busch Gardens Tampa
Location: United States
Type: Steel
Opened: 1993
Designer/Manufacturer: Werner Stengel/Bolliger & Mabillard
Height (ft): 143
Drop (ft): 135
Speed (mph): 60
Inversions: 7
Video: https://www.youtube.com/watch?v=QVrVpURcgkw

Kumba has been wowing guests in the Congo section of Busch Gardens Tampa since 1993. The Bolliger and Mabillard steel coaster is named for the African Congo word for "roar," which is a fitting name given the loud roaring sound the coaster makes as it careens through the course (caused by the rectangular-shaped spine of the coaster track, a signature feature of B&M coasters). Kumba was designed by notable roller coaster designer Warner Stengel, and takes riders 143 feet into the air, which made it the tallest roller coaster in Florida when it opened in 1993 (a record it later conceded to Montu, a B&M inverted coaster built on the other side of the park). After a 135-foot drop, riders traverse through 7 inversions and nearly 4,000 feet of coaster track during the ride's 3:00 experience. Kumba features a 108-foot-high vertical loop that travels around the lift hill, which was also a record in 1993 though the height record was later surpassed by the 118-foot loop on PortAventura's Dragon Khan. Kumba is one of only three roller coasters in the world with a loop around the lift hill, and was the first roller coaster to feature this element. (Riddler's Revenge at Six Flags Magic Mountain, and now Banshee at Kings Island are the other two.) Kumba also features a set of iconic interlocking corkscrews that seem to be one of the most photographed portions of the coaster.

Kumba consistently scores well in *Amusement Today's*

Golden Ticket Awards for top steel roller coaster, and is one of only seven roller coasters that has been ranked in the top 50 every year since the awards were created in 1998 (ranking as high as 4 in 1998, and bottoming out at 31 in 2011).

Kumba was just the sixth roller coaster to be designed and built by the now-famous Swiss firm. The high capacity and smoothness of the ride firmly cemented the fledgling company as the best roller coaster manufacturer in the world. To date, Bolliger and Mabillard have produced 97 roller coasters, but it was Kumba that proved to the amusement industry that B&M could design more than just gimmicky stand-up or inverted coasters, and that they were here to stay.

11. THE RACER

Known for: Vital part of the roller coaster renaissance of the 1970s
Park: Kings Island
Location: United States
Type: Wood
Opened: 1972
Designer/Manufacturer: John C. Allen/Philadelphia Toboggan
Coasters
Height (ft): 88
Drop (ft): 82.17
Speed (mph): 53
Video: https://www.youtube.com/watch?v=4IPtcbwz_YO

To understand The Racer's importance in the history of the roller coaster, we have to go back to the 1920s, which were considered to be the "Golden Age" of roller coasters in America. An estimated 2,000 wooden coasters were built before the Great Depression reversed the process. The amusement industry was hit hard during the '30s and '40s, and continued to struggle through the '50s and '60s. Depression, wars, and social unrest were all factors in the decline of the amusement park.

In 1972, The Racer at Kings Island in Mason, Ohio, sparked a renewed interest in amusement parks and ushered in the "Second Golden Age" of wooden roller coasters. The classic designed by John C. Allen was an integral part of Kings Island when it opened on May 27, 1972. The Racer's two tracks were laid out side-by-side in an out-and-back fashion. Originally, both trains faced forward, but in 1982 one side was turned around to face backward.

One of the few original attractions still operating today, the Racer's white-latticed structure dominates the Coney Mall section of the park. The out-and-back coaster was featured on an episode of *The Brady Bunch*, and inspired similar designs in other roller coasters around the world, such as Rebel Yell at Kings Dominion and Thunder Road at Carowinds.

10. MILLENNIUM FORCE

Known for: World's first giga-coaster
Park: Cedar Point
Location: United States
Type: Steel
Opened: 2000
Designer/Manufacturer: Werner Stengel/Intamin
Height (ft): 310
Drop (ft): 300
Speed (mph): 93
Video: https://www.youtube.com/watch?v=jbXPhOFRxTc

The coaster world was taken by storm with the stunning announcement of Millennium Force at Cedar Point. The biggest investment in the park's storied history would be the first roller coaster with a complete circuit to break the 300-foot mark (though its record would be broken a few months later by Steel Dragon 2000). The ride's stats were ridiculous, and had coaster enthusiasts all over the world salivating: 310 feet tall, 80° drop, 93 mph, and over 6,000 feet of track. The last hill on Millennium Force is taller than a large majority of other coasters. A ride this size was unheard of at the time.

Millennium Force would pave the way for a new era in coasters and employed new technology. Millennium Force was the first to use a cable lift to quickly pull the nine car trains up its mammoth 310-foot tall lift hill in 22 seconds. A relatively new variation on the chain lift, the cable system allowed for a faster and steeper lift hill, which is often quiet because the anti-rollback devices are electromagnetically disengaged by the passing train and automatically close after it passes. The cable is connected to a catch car that rides on its own guide in the middle of the track. The catch car attaches underneath the vehicle so that, as the cable is wound up on a giant drum, the train is pulled to the top of the lift hill.

Millennium Force graces the top of many coaster enthusiasts best ride lists, and is often considered the best roller coaster in the world. It was briefly the tallest and fastest until Steel

Dragon 2000 opened later the same year. It paved the way for larger rides, including Top Thrill Dragster, which came just three years later. It's still the second-longest roller coaster in North America, after The Beast at Kings Island. Since its debut, Millennium Force has been voted the number one steel roller coaster nine times in *Amusement Today's* Golden Ticket Awards. Its lowest ranking in the poll has been second, a position that it has swapped with Bizarro at Six Flags New England numerous times over the years.

9. AERIAL WALK

Known for: First full-circuit coaster
Location: France
Type: Wood
Opened: 1817

A French businessman that rode Russia's ice slides wanted to bring the slides back to France. The climate wasn't quite as cold, so the slides could not be operated all year long. The solution was to add wheels to the sleds and forgo the need for ice. This didn't make the rides any safer, but at least they could now operate all year long.

The Aerial Walk (also known as Promenades Aeriennes) featured a heart-shaped layout with two tracks that flowed in opposite directions from a central tower. The cars followed grooves in the track. The Aerial Walk was a key moment in the history of the roller coaster, and set the stage for future rides.

8. THE CENTRIFUGAL RAILWAY

Known for: First known looping coaster
Park: Frascati Garden
Location: France
Type: Wood
Opened: 1840
Designer/Manufacturer: Clavieres; Hutchinson, Higgins, et al.
Height (ft): 43
Drop (ft): 43
Inversions: 1

Soon after roller coasters evolved from ice slides to wheeled carts rolling down tracks, amusement park owners dreamed of inverting customers upside down. The Centrifugal Railway was the first known looping coaster. The design was actually created in 1833 by an engineer named Clavieres, but it was not implemented into a functioning ride until a decade later. By today's standards, this ride would have been known as a shuttle coaster: there was no lift hill or launch, and the track was not a complete circuit. The entire coaster was essentially one 43-foot drop into the 13-foot diameter loop, followed by a small rise up to the unloading platform. The coaster had no upstop wheels or other way to lock it to the track. It relied on pure centrifugal force to not fly off, hence the name Centrifugal Railway.

But the extreme forces on the ride made for an uncomfortable experience. It was said riders felt as many as 12Gs when going through the vertical loop. As engineers would figure out later on, the shape of the loop determines how much force is felt by the passengers at different locations along the loop, so the perfect circle design was not very good. Looping riders weren't made entirely safe until Corkscrew and Revolution, which we'll get to soon.

7. MAUCH CHUNK RAILWAY
Known for: America's first roller coaster
Location: United States
Opened: 1827
Closed: 1930s
Designer/Manufacturer: Lehigh Coal & Navigation Company

The roller coaster evolution really began to accelerate when these unique machines were introduced in the United States. America's first roller coaster was actually more of a railroad that doubled as a thrill ride. The 3.5-foot narrow gauge Mauch Chunk Switchback Railway, or Mauch Chunk & Summit Hill Railway, was built in 1827 by the Lehigh Coal & Navigation Company

36—" Switch-back " Railroad, Mauch Chunk, Pa., U. S. A.

(LC&N) in the mountains of Pennsylvania. Its primary purpose was to deliver coal from the mountains down to the Lehigh River. The track grew to be 18 miles long, and in 1873 it became more popular as a ride than coal hauler, carrying only paying passengers. In fact, it carried over 35,000 eager passengers in one year. The cost of an 80-minute ride was only one dollar.

6. DROP-THE-DIPS

Known for: First to use lap bar restraints
Park: Coney Island
Location: United States
Type: Wood
Opened: 1907
Closed: 1930
Designer/Manufacturer: Mosley/Chris Feucht
Height (ft): 60

Roller coaster restraints come in all shapes and sizes, but generally fall into two categories: lap bars or over-the-shoulder. Lap bars are U-shaped devices connected to the floor that rest on the riders' laps, securing them by the legs. Over-the-shoulder harnesses are mounted behind the rider and swing down over the shoulders. Both systems usually use a standard seat belt as a redundant fail safe. Another feature the types of restraints have in common is only one degree of freedom, meaning movement is only allowed in one axis, a rotation. Having only one degree of freedom makes it easy for the control system to know the exact position of the restraint with respect to the rider. A go/no-go sensor tells the ride operator if the restraint is in the correct closed position before the coaster can be dispatched.

The first roller coaster to make use of lap bar restraints was the Drop-the-Dips in 1907 at Coney Island in Brooklyn, New York. The addition of a passenger-restraining device allowed for wilder rides with zero or negative g-forces. Previous coasters may have used a simple chain or strap across riders' legs, and often had no restraining device at all other than physics. Gentle slopes and only positive g-forces held passengers in their seats. That is until Drop-the-Dips used a solid bar, ushering in an age of steeper and faster rides.

5. THOMPSON'S SWITCHBACK RAILWAY

Known for: First coaster designed as an amusement ride in America
Park: Coney Island
Location: United States
Type: Wood
Opened: 1884
Designer/Manufacturer: LaMarcus Adna Thompson
Height (ft): 50
Drop (ft): 43
Speed (mph): 6
Video: https://www.youtube.com/watch?v=86qKAoVdKYo

The single most influential figure in the evolution of the roller coaster is LaMarcus Adna Thompson. Inspired by the Mauch Chunk Switchback Railroad, Thompson started designing his own shorter version, which opened at New York's Coney Island park on June 13, 1884 as The La Marcus Thompson Switchback Railway. It consisted of two side-by-side, 50-foot tall tracks that went in opposite directions. Once a car reached the bottom of one side it could be hauled up to the top of the other to make the return trip. Passengers left the train and attendants pushed the cars over a switch to the higher level before the passengers returned to their seats and completed the journey back to the starting point. The track was 600 feet long and cars traveled at six mph.

Despite its lack of speed, people would still wait over three hours to ride the coaster, which became extremely popular almost overnight. Admission to the ride was a nickel, raising a profit of $600 per day. Because of the success of The La Marcus Thompson Switchback Railway, Thompson started building his railways worldwide with different themes. Thompson is known today as the "Father of Gravity" for his contributions to the roller coaster industry.

4. CORKSCREW

Known for: First modern steel inverting roller coaster
Park: Knott's Berry Farm
Location: United States
Type: Steel
Opened: 1975
Relocated: 1989
Designer/Manufacturer:
Ron Toomer/Arrow Dynamics
Height (ft): 72
Drop (ft): 62
Speed (mph): 32
Inversions: 2
Video:
https://www.youtube.com/watch?v=
hNyuHth9pjE

Engineers have always dreamed of making a roller coaster go upside down, but previous attempts had resulted in unsafe or uncomfortable rides. Almost all of the previous efforts had tried to use a circular vertical loop, a very high G type of inversion. Ron Toomer and Arrow Dynamics decided to find a solution by changing the shape of the inversion. They took each end of the loop and stretched it out into what is today commonly known as a corkscrew. A prototype was built at Arrow Dynamics's manufacturing facility in Mountain View, California (before they relocated to Utah). When management from Knott's Berry Farm theme park rode the prototype they decided they had to have one for their park.

When it opened in 1975, Corkscrew would become the first modern inverting roller coaster, as well as the first to go upside down twice. The ride was an instant hit. Ten exact replicas were produced between 1975 and 1979. In 1989, the land-limited Knott's Berry Farm sold the Corkscrew to Silverwood Theme Park in Idaho for $250,000 to make room for the new Boomerang coaster. You can still ride this important piece of coaster history at Silverwood today.

3. MAGNUM XL-200

Known for: First coaster to break 200-foot mark
Park: Cedar Point
Location: United States
Type: Steel
Opened: 1989
Designer/Manufacturer: Ron Toomer/Arrow Dynamics
Height (ft): 205
Drop (ft): 194.7
Speed (mph): 72
Video: https://www.youtube.com/watch?v=EzBlkPdJ2lc

Magnum XL-200 opened in 1989 and was the first roller coaster to break the 200-foot tall mark. Interestingly, a 1989 park brochure listed the ride's height at only 201 feet, versus the 205-foot-tall statistic seen today. The 201-foot statistic came from the ride's blueprints and did not account for the height of the footers (the cement foundations that stick out of the ground) the coaster sits on.

Magnum is a traditional out-and-back coaster featuring 5,106 feet of track that winds its way over the neighboring Soak City waterpark and along the shores of Lake Erie, giving riders a breathtaking view. This is surely one of the best locations of any coaster. Since 1989, Magnum has given more than 36 million guests a ride to remember. In 2006 alone, 1,826,338 guests rode Magnum.

As impressive as the numbers are, coaster enthusiasts will tell you the element that makes Magnum truly terrifying is its airtime—that incredible feeling of floating over each of the ride's intense bunny hills. For safety purposes, riders must be at least 48 inches tall.

Magnum cemented Cedar Point's reputation as the "Roller Coaster Capital of the World." It proved you could build a ride over 200 feet tall, and that a large steel roller coaster didn't have to go upside down to be exciting or exhilarating. In 2006, the Magnum XL-200 was voted number three in the "Best Steel Roller Coaster in the World" category in a poll conducted by *Amusement Today*. The lowest it's ever placed in the Golden Ticket Awards is 13[th.]

2. REVOLUTION
Known for: First roller coaster with a modern (clothoid) loop
Park: Six Flags Magic Mountain
Location: United States
Type: Steel
Opened: 1976
Designer/Manufacturer: Werner Stengel/Anton Schwarzkopf
Height (ft): 113
Drop (ft): 85
Speed (mph): 55
Inversions: 1
Video: https://www.youtube.com/watch?v=78GGr4Mv97s

Vertical loop inversions were finally made safe and comfortable by Werner Stengel in 1975. He ditched the perfect circle and designed a loop with a radius of curvature that decreases as the vehicles are turned upside down. Stengel realized coaster trains are faster at the bottom of loops and slower at the top, just like when they traverse an airtime hill. The shape of a loop determines how much force is felt by the passengers at different locations along the loop. Centrifugal force pushes out from the center, while centripetal force keeps an object in its circular path (gravity for an orbiting satellite, for example). Centripetal force is the same force that prevents water from falling out of a bucket that is swung upside down on a string.

Werner Stengel created a safe and smooth vertical loop by gradually decreasing the radius of the track using an Euler spiral or clothoid (or klothoide, pronounced "clockoid") configuration. Clothoids are frequently used in railways, road building, and highway exits. While the upper part of the vertical loop is a half circle, the lower part has a completely different shape—that of a "Cornu spiral," where the radius of curvature increases as you get closer to the ground. The clothoid shape leads to a slower onset of lower forces on the body by keeping the G forces at the top of the loop close to those of the bottom, leading to a much safer and more enjoyable ride for passengers (and no broken bones)!

The first roller coaster with a modern (clothoid) loop was Revolution at Six Flags Magic Mountain. The steel coaster opened on May 8, 1976, 200 years after the American Revolution for which it was named. Revolution is an ACE Coaster Landmark, though if the opening had been delayed, the ride would not have been as significant. Eight days later, Corkscrew opened at Cedar Point on May 15, 1976, with a vertical loop and two corkscrews for a total of three inversions.

1. MATTERHORN BOBSLEDS

Known for: First tubular steel continuous track roller coaster
Park: Disneyland
Location: United States
Type: Steel
Opened: 1959
Designer/Manufacturer: WED Enterprises/Arrow Dynamics
Height (ft): 80
Speed (mph): 27
Video: www.youtube.com/watch?v=mtfmzH4Exbc

Roller coasters had been around for nearly 150 years before the Matterhorn Bobsleds completely changed the game in 1959. Other steel roller coasters had been built, but Disney's coaster was the first to use tubular steel rails. The strength and versatility of steel track and support systems lead to more innovative designs and seating configurations.

Thanks to this innovation, the 1990s saw a massive surge in steel roller coaster creation leading historians to call it the "Golden Age of Steel Coasters." Today, a majority of roller coasters are classified as "steel" rather than "wooden." According to the Roller Coaster Database, there are approximately 3,000 roller coasters operating worldwide today. Of these, only 172 (or 6.14%) are classified as "wood" coasters. The difference is primarily based on the material that the rails are constructed from, and not what the supports are made of.

A steel roller coaster is usually completely fabricated from steel, including the rails and supports, and the total material weight can be over a thousand tons. Tubular steel rails are formed by heating and then permanently bending steel pipe into the desired shape by running straight pieces of steel through a series of rollers. The difficulty is that metal bends at either its weakest point or where the strongest force is applied over a span. For a smooth ride the rails need to be extremely precise, within a tenth of a millimeter of their designed shape. For this reason, track manufacturers are very secretive about their exact steel bending processes. Today's modern steel looping behemoths can be directly traced back to the Matterhorn Bobsleds.

The coaster, in typical Disney fashion, is heavily themed. The faux mountain it resides in is modeled after the Matterhorn, a real mountain in the Swiss Alps. It employs forced perspective to seem more impressively large. Throughout the day, climbers dressed in Swiss mountain-climbing garb may be seen scaling the peak, often accompanied by Disney characters such as Mickey Mouse and Goofy. A sky ride is also used to pass through the center of the mountain.

The Matterhorn also pioneered control systems by being the first coaster to safely allow multiple trains to operate on the same track at the same time, due to the use of individual brake zones (called blocks). Another amazing fact is that, despite being the first of its kind, the ride was designed and built in less than a year—an incredible feat considering paper and not computers was used for the design process!

The Matterhorn also helped pave the way for the modern looping roller coasters of the 1970s. Many others soon followed, and for this reason it's been designated an ACE (American Coaster Enthusiasts) Coaster Landmark. The most important roller coaster ever built hasn't even seen its 60th birthday yet, which shows you how far roller coaster design has come in such a short time—in large part due to the computer.

Ground-breaking Coaster Statistics

Where are (or were) these fifty historic scream machines located? The majority of groundbreaking roller coasters are found in the United States and Europe. Currently, there's only one on the list from China and Brazil respectively. However, in the future I expect this number to increase. The complete breakdown by country:

United States: 38
United Kingdom: 3
France: 2
Belgium: 1
Brazil: 1
China: 1
Denmark: 1
Japan: 1
Netherlands: 1
UAE: 1
Russia: Unknown

Kings Island in Mason, Ohio was amazingly home to six of these roller coasters, or 12% of the list. Sadly, only three are left standing today (The Beast, Flight of Fear, and the Racer – the current Bat coaster is not the original). Other notable parks are Six Flags Magic Mountain with four, Coney Island with four, Cedar Point has three, and Alton Towers, Six Flags Great Adventure, and Kings Dominion all have two on the list.

Who builds the most groundbreaking roller coasters? Probably the most famous roller coaster company has been Arrow Dynamics, with six coasters on the list, and three out of the top five. The number increases to seven if you count S&S Worldwide coasters, the company that eventually bought out Arrow after they declared for bankruptcy. Intamin, a company well-known for taking risks and pushing the limits of coaster design, has five coasters on this list, followed by B&M with four. The complete breakdown:

Arrow Dynamics: 6

Intamin: 5

B&M: 4

Gerstlauer: 2

Rocky Mountain Construction: 2

Vekoma: 2

Morgan: 2

RCCA: 2

CCI: 2

TGG: 2

S&S: 1

TOGO: 1

Premier: 1

PTC: 1

Type

Steel: 28

Wood: 22

Status

Currently operating: 32

Defunct: 18

Features

Number that go upside down: 16

Number that feature a launch segment: 8

Not a complete circuit: 5

1800s: 4

1900s: 31

2000s: 15

Most Innovative Years

2000: 3

2002: 3

2013: 3

1996: 2

1997: 2

1999: 2

Narrowly Missed the List

It's difficult to select a list of fifty roller coasters out of literally tens of thousands. Here are a few that just missed the cut:

- ❖ Thirteen at Alton Towers - The first coaster with a vertical freefall drop section.
- ❖ Furius Baco at Port Adventura – The first wing coaster.
- ❖ Maximum RPM at Hard Rock Park – First coaster to use a Ferris wheel lift.
- ❖ Tower of Terror at Dreamworld – First coaster to break 100mph.
- ❖ Space Mountain – Disneyland Paris – First use of on-board audio
- ❖ Gravity Pleasure at Coney Island – First use of a powered chain lift.

The Best and Worst Years for Roller Coasters

2015 is going to be a great year for new roller coasters here in the United States. Two rides in particular, Wicked Cyclone at Six Flags New England and Fury 325 at Carowinds, will have a legitimate shot at being one of the best roller coasters in the world. And you've still got the incredible looking Twisted Colossus at Six Flags Magic Mountain and the interesting Cannibal at Lagoon. Oh, and don't forget about Batman: The Ride, Impulse, Tempesto, and Laff Trakk.

2015 may be one of the best years for new roller coasters in America ever. However, we won't be able to fully judge it until all the new rides open and operate successfully. But that got me thinking: Besides 2015, what year had the best coaster "class" ever? If the 1920s were the golden age of wood coasters, and the '70s ushered in a second golden age, has there been a third golden age? What years were the best ever for coaster fans?

To come up with the list of top five coaster "classes," I used the following determining factors to try and be as objective and impartial as possible:

Quantity of new rides: I looked up the total number of new roller coasters opened per year according to the Roller Coaster Data Base (http://www.rcdb.com).

Quality of new rides: I looked at the last Mitch Hawker polls from 2013 (he does separate wood (http://ushsho.com/woodrollercoasterpollresults2013.htm) and steel polls (http://ushsho.com/detailedsteelrollercoasterpollresults2013.htm).

Innovation: Was technology pushed forward or were the rides all proven models?

Historical significance: How big of an impact did a coaster have, regardless of whether it was actually good or not?

Based on this criteria, here are the top five best years for new roller coasters in America:

5. Class of 2012
Total number of new coasters: 23
Currently in Top 100: 4 (5 if you include Leviathan)
Mitch's 2013 Steel Coaster Poll Top 100: 2
Mitch Hawker 2013 Wood Coaster Poll Top 100: 0
Notable coasters: Skyrush, Wild Eagle, X-Flight, Manta, Verbolten

2012 saw the addition of several unique types of coasters. Wild Eagle and X Flight, the first wing coasters in America, opened. Verbolten was the first US coaster with a vertical dropping track segment. SeaWorld San Diego opened Manta, the first Mack launched coaster in the US. And SkyRush at Hershey Park may be the most extreme steel coaster in the US (#5 in Mitch's 2013 steel poll).

4. Class of 1998
Total number of new coasters: 50
Currently in Top 100: 4
Mitch's 2013 Steel Coaster Poll Top 100: 2
Mitch Hawker 2013 Wood Coaster Poll Top 100: 3
Notable coasters: Shivering Timbers, Volcano, Mr. Freeze, Great Bear, Mamba, Riddler's Revenge, Roar, Twisted Twins

1998 was a really solid year. The quantity of new coasters was very high, but the quality was not quite as good as the other classes. Shivering Timbers at Michigan's Adventure is one of the biggest wooden coasters, and highly rated. A pair of Mr. Freeze LIM launch coasters opened as well. Twisted Twins was a new dueling wooden coaster for Kentucky Kingdom, and Riddler's Revenge is the pinnacle of the stand-up coaster model.

3. Class of 2001
Total number of new coasters: 39
Currently in Top 100: 7
Mitch's 2013 Steel Coaster Poll Top 100: 5
Mitch Hawker 2013 Wood Coaster Poll Top 100: 1
Notable coasters: Nitro, Phantom's Revenge, Talon, Titan, Cornball Express, Wildfire, California Screamin', X-Flight (Geauga Lake), Deja Vu, Hypersonix XLC

After a stellar coaster season in 2000, one might have expected a large drop off the following year. On the contrary, 2001's coaster class is almost as good as the one that preceded it. Deja Vu and Hypersonic XLC were two new innovative creations that, while not successful in the long term, did keep pushing technology and the industry forward. And Phantom's Revenge may have been the template to show parks that you can retrofit an existing ride to take it from good to great.

2. Class of 2006
Total number of new coasters: 32
Currently in Top 100: 7 (4 in the top 50)
Mitch's 2013 Steel Coaster Poll Top 100: 2
Mitch Hawker 2013 Wood Coaster Poll Top 100: 3
Notable coasters: The Voyage, El Toro, Goliath, Tatsu, Kentucky Rumbler, Expedition Everest, Patriot

2006's class is ranked number two for two main reasons: The Voyage and El Toro. Ask any coaster enthusiast what their favorite ride is and chances are it's one of these two. They've both held the number one spot in the poll. You also have what may be the best flying roller coaster ever built in Tatsu. And it's a good year anytime Disney opens a new coaster, as they're few and far between.

1. Class of 2000
Total number of new coasters: 60

Currently in Top 100: 11 (6 rides in the top 50)
Mitch's 2013 Steel Coaster Poll Top 100: 8
Mitch Hawker 2013 Wood Coaster Poll Top 100: 4
Notable coasters: Millennium Force, Goliath, Son of Beast, Superman (New England), Kraken, Stealth, Villain, Legend, Boulder Dash, Lightning Racer

The year 2000 was by far the best year for new roller coasters ever, not just in quantity, but quality as well. Two of the most beloved steel roller coasters ever built opened this year with Millennium Force and Six Flag New England's Superman. You can argue whether or not Son of Beast was a good ride (it wasn't), but you can't argue its historical significance and the impact it had (park guests still talk about it). An incredible five roller coasters stood over 200 feet tall, and that's not including Steel Dragon 2000. Technology was pushed with looping wooden coasters, a cable lift on Millennium Force, and the opening of Stealth, the first successful flying roller coaster. Living in Ohio at the time felt like being at the center of it all with Millennium Force, Son of Beast, and Six Flags Ohio. Ironically, Millennium Force is the only thing still operating in the state. Yes, 2015 will be a good year, but 2000 may never be topped.

Honorable Mention: Classes of 1996, 1999

There you have it—the top five best coaster classes. Looking back, it's pretty obvious that 1998–2001 was a very special time. It's crazy that three of these classes occurred during a four-year period—another golden age of roller coasters for sure.

Now, let's look at the other end of the spectrum: the top five worst classes of new roller coasters. As with the last list, I've tried my best to be as objective and impartial as possible, but this time I'd say the quantity of new coasters was the biggest influence, along with quality, innovation, and historical significance. Here are the top five worst years for new roller coasters in America:

5. Class of 2003
Total number of new coasters: 28
Notable coaster: Top Thrill Dragster at Cedar Point

For most of our readers, this may be the only coaster class on this list they were even alive for. Top Thrill Dragster was the highlight of the year by far, but former Cedar Fair CEO Dick Kinzel said it was probably the worst business decision he's ever made (http://www.npr.org/templates/story/story.php?storyId=4990536). The majority of the other new coasters built in 2003 were all clones, or copies of existing rides (e.g., Steel Venom, Superman Ultimate Flight (x2), Batman the Ride) or parking lot coasters like Scream at Six Flags Magic Mountain (also a clone).

4. Class of 1983
Total number of new coasters: 7
Notable coaster: Cyclone at Six Flags New England

Yes, the most notable roller coaster opened in 1983 was Cyclone at Six Flags New England, the same ride that was just closed in 2014. That's pretty sad.

3. Class of 1982
Total number of new coasters: 6
Notable coaster: Viper at Darien Lake and Grizzly at Kings Dominion

Viper at Darien Lake is one of two coasters you've probably heard of that opened in 1982. In the 2013 Mitch Hawker Steel Coaster Poll (http://ushsho.com/detailedsteelrollercoasterpollresults2013.htm), Viper came in at 311, out of 364 steel coasters. Grizzly at Kings Dominion was rated 104th "best" wood coaster in the 2013 Mitch Hawker Wood Coaster Poll (http://ushsho.com/detailedwoodrollercoasterpollresults2013.htm) – out of 175.

2. Tie between class of 1932 and 1945

Total number of new coasters each year: 1

Notable coaster: Giant Racer at Saltair, Cyclone at Palisades (not the Traver-designed Cyclone)

Only one new coaster was built in 1932 and 1945 respectively. But this should come as no surprise. In 1945, World War II was still wrapping up, and 1932 was in the midst of the Great Depression. Giant Racer opened at Saltair, an amusement park in Salt Lake City. Also, in the 1940s theme parks were associated with cheap forms of entertainment. In 1939 there were only 245 coasters operating worldwide.

1. Tie between class of 1943 and 1944

Total number of new coasters each year: 0

Notable coasters None:

Yes, no new roller coasters were opened between the years of 1943 and 1944. Not surprising, seeing as how the United States (and most of the world) were fighting in a world war. If you were a roller coaster enthusiast back then, you were probably fighting in the war, but if not, it was a long wait until a new coaster opened.

Honorable mention: 1985 is saved from being in the top five by the opening of the Phoenix at Knoebels.

There was a lot going on in the world, so the 1930s and '40s have a good reason why so few coasters were built: lack of business due to depression, and lack of building materials. The 1980s were a rough time (literally, with all the Arrow coasters), until B&M came onto the scene in 1990 with their super smooth rides. 2003 was also rather disappointing, especially considering how awesome 1998–2001 were.

Legacy of the Roller Coaster

Roller coasters exist to provide us with a break from everyday life. They create an exhilarating—and often addicting—distraction from the experiences your senses are used to. The feeling of being out of control without any real danger is not easy to come by. Humans, by nature, are programmed to go looking for danger. Skydiving, mountaineering, and racing are just a few of the many sports man indulges in just for the thrill of it. Not everyone is such a daredevil, however, and with the use of appropriate technologies, people are now enjoying these thrills without the danger. Roller coasters are a perfect example of ingenious use of technology. Pick your amusement park, anywhere on the planet, and where are the longest, most aggravating lines? The roller coasters, of course! They are the main attractions on the midways these days, with millions strapping themselves into these scream machines because they love being scared in a safe environment. The success of a ride can easily be measured in smiles!

Roller coaster fanatics are constantly craving taller, faster, longer, and more intense thrill rides. Upon each visit to the amusement park, the ante must be upped. Parks look to innovate, to one-up their competitors. "World's first" is the most popular marketing strategy today. Theme parks will take financial risks for something no one else in the world has done, and the fans will travel from all over to brave it. The challenge for the designers is to make the experiences ever more extreme while maintaining the same standards of safety.

Roller coasters come in a mind-blowing profusion of styles. Some are successful and will eventually be replicated in the future. Others are unique because, well, the idea wasn't very good. Or too expensive to maintain. What coaster will go down in history next as an innovation, or a turning point? What model will be cloned multiple times and installed on multiple continents? More coasters will be built as the industry turns from China to India and Brazil. Roller coaster designers are constantly innovating and pushing the limits. The roller coasters of tomorrow will look far different than the thrill rides of today. No matter what, the end of the roller coaster's evolution is, thankfully, nowhere in sight. I look forward to riding the next milestone in the evolution of the roller coaster, wherever and whenever that will be.

Would You Like to Know More About Roller Coaster Design?

Have you ever wondered what it takes to design and build a roller coaster? At last, there's a book that shows you. A mix of engineering and art, roller coasters are complex three-dimensional puzzles consisting of thousands of individual parts. Designers spend countless hours creating and tweaking ride paths to push the envelope of exhilaration, all while maintaining the highest safety standards. *Coasters 101: An Engineering Guide to Roller Coaster Design* examines the numerous diverse aspects of roller coaster engineering, including some of the mathematical formulas and engineering concepts used.

A few of the topics covered include:

- ❖ Design Software and Computer Technology
- ❖ Project Management
- ❖ Wheel Design and Material Selection
- ❖ Track Fabrication Techniques
- ❖ Daily Inspections and Preventive Maintenance
- ❖ Amusement Industry Safety Standards
- ❖ Career Advice

And much more!

This technical guide is the most detailed roller coaster design book to date and will take you through the entire process, from concept to creation. A must read for every enthusiast and aspiring roller coaster engineer!

Get **Coasters 101: An Engineering Guide to Roller Coaster Design** from Amazon.com today.

Did You Like 50 Groundbreaking Roller Coasters?

Before you go, I'd like to say "thank you" for purchasing my book. I know you could have picked from dozens of other books but you took a chance on mine. So a big thanks for ordering this book and reading all the way to the end.

Now I'd like to ask for a *small* favor. Could you please take a minute or two and leave a review for this book on Amazon.com? Your comments are really valuable because they will guide future editions of this book and I'm always striving to improve my writing.

About the Author

Nick Weisenberger is currently co-manager of Coaster101.com as well as a member of the ASTM International F-24 committee on Amusement Rides and Devices. He's ridden over one hundred and fifty different coasters and in August 2009, he participated in the Coasting for Kids Ride-a-thon where he endured a ten hour marathon ride (that's 105 laps) and helped raise over $10,000 for Give Kids the World charity. When not writing or working, Nick likes to read, hike, watch football, and explore. An avid traveler, look for Nick on the midways of your local amusement park!

What to know more? Drop by and check out Coaster101.com, a growing resource and community for roller coaster enthusiasts, aspiring students, and theme park fans.

Questions or comments? Email me: **nick@coaster101.com**

Or feel free to say hi on Twitter (@NTWProductions).

Works by Nick Weisenberger

Coasters 101: An Engineer's Guide to Roller Coaster Design

The 50 Most *Terrifying* Roller Coasters Ever Built

The 50 Most *Unique* Roller Coasters Ever Built

The 50 Biggest Ferris Wheels Ever Built

50 Legendary Roller Coasters That No Longer Exist

Coaster Phobia: How to Overcome Your Fear of Roller Coasters

Things to Do in the Smokies with Kids

Once I was Adopted

Appendix I: Glossary

4th Dimension: Controlled rotatable seats cantilevered on each side of the track.

Airtime: Roller coasters can thrust negative Gs on riders causing them to momentarily lift off their seats and become "weightless." As the vehicle flies over the top of a hill the load on the passenger becomes less than Earth's gravity and, in the extreme, could throw an unrestrained passenger out of the car. Scream machines with oodles of so-called "airtime" moments or "butterflies in your stomach" thrills rank among the world's best. Negative g-forces cannot be too great because when under high negative g forces blood rushed to the head and can cause "red out."

Block: A block is a section of a roller coaster's track with a controllable start and stop point. Only one train may occupy a block at a time.

Bobsled: Cars travel freely down a U-shaped track (no rails) like a bobsled except on wheels.

Bunny Hops: A series of small hills engineered to give repeated doses of airtime

Cobra roll: A half-loop followed by half a corkscrew, then another half corkscrew into another half-loop. The trains are inverted twice and exit the element the opposite direction in which they entered.

Corkscrew: A loop where the entrance and exit points have been stretched apart.

Cycle: When the train completes one circuit around the course. When trains are run continuously this is called cycling.

Dark ride: An indoor ride, usually slow moving through sets based on a central theme, sometime will feature interactivity like shooting at targets

Dive loop: The track twists upward and to the side, similar to half a corkscrew, before diving towards the ground in a half-loop. Basically, the opposite of an Immelman inversion.

Dueling: Two separate tracks but mostly not parallel. Usually contain several head-on, near miss collision sensations.

Floorless: The vehicle sits above the track but contains no floor between the rider's feet and the rails, allowing their legs to dangle freely.

G force: G force is expressed as a ratio of the force developed in changing speed or direction relative to the force felt due to the Earth's gravity. The smaller the curve radius and the higher the speed, the greater the g-force felt. Thus, a 2g force on a 100 pound body causes it to weigh 200 pounds (Weight = Mass x G Force). Indianapolis 500 racers are subjected to more than 3g's in the corners of their hairpin turns while there are looping coasters that subject passengers to as much as 6g's. Positive g-forces, meaning those that push your butt into the seat, become uncomfortable for the human body at +5g and may cause the loss of consciousness.

Giga coaster: Any roller coaster with at least one element between 300 and 399 feet tall.

Hyper coaster: Any roller coaster with at least one element between 200 and 299 feet tall.

Imagineer: A person who works for Walt Disney Imagineering. This word is a combination of engineer and imagination.

Immelman: Named after the aircraft maneuver pioneered by Max Immelman, the inversion begins with a vertical loop but at the apex of the inversion turns into a corkscrew exiting at the side instead of completing the loop. The opposite of a dive loop element.

Inversion: An element on a roller coaster track which turns riders 180 degrees upside down and then rights them again, such as a loop, corkscrew, or barrel roll (among others).

Inverted: Vehicle is fixed below the rails with rider's feet hanging freely and is able to invert upside down.

Laydown/Flying: Riders are parallel to the rails, either on their back or stomach.

Mobius: A racing or dueling roller coaster with one continuous track instead of two separate ones.

Motorbike: Riders straddle the seats as if riding a motorcycle, jet ski, or horse.

Pipeline: Riders are positioned between the rails instead of above or below them.

Queue: A line you stand in for an attraction, food, or entry/exit.

Racing Coaster: Two separate tracks usually parallel for most of the course. Trains are released simultaneously so they race from start to finish.

Sit down: Traditional roller coaster with vehicles above the rails.

Spinning: Seats can freely spin on a horizontal axis.

Standup: Riders are restrained in a standing position.

Swinging suspended: The vehicle hangs below the rails and can freely swing from side to side but does not invert.

Themed: The central idea or concept for an attraction or area.

THRC: Theoretical Hourly Ride Capacity is the number of guests per hour that can experience an attraction under optimal operating conditions. Calculated by: Riders per bench*benches per car*cars per train*(60min/ride time minutes).

Wingrider: The seats are fixed on both sides of the vehicle outside of the rails.

Appendix II: Acronyms

The following is a list of acronyms found within this text and includes common terms used throughout the amusement industry (in alphabetical order).

ACE: American Coaster Enthusiasts
ARB: Anti-Roll Back
ASTM: American Society of Standards and Materials
CAD: Computer Aided Design
CPM: Critical Path Method
FEA: Finite Element Analysis
FMEA: Failure Mode and Effects Analysis
FTA: Fault Tree Analysis
GDT: Geometrical Dimension and Tolerance
IAAPA: International Association of Amusement Parks and Attractions
ISO: International Organization for Standardization
LIM: Linear Induction Motor
LOTO: Lock Out Tag Out
LSM: Linear Synchronous Motor
MBD: Model Based Definition
MTBF: Mean Time Between Failures
MTTR: Mean Time To Repair
OEM: Original Equipment Manufacturer
OSHA: Occupational Safety and Health Administration
OSS: Operator Safety System
PERT: Project Evaluation and Review Technique
PLC: Programmable Logic Controller
POV: Point of View
RA: Ride Analysis
RAC: Ride Access Control
RCDB: Roller Coaster Data Base
SBNO: Standing But Not Operating
SLC: Suspended Looping Coaster
SRCS: Safety Related Control Systems
T&A: Test and Adjust
THRC: Theoretical Hourly Ride Capacity

Appendix III: Notable Dates in Roller Coaster History

1400 - First known roller coaster

1600 - Russian ice slides

1784 - First coaster on wheels built in the Gardens of Oreinabum in St. Petersburg, Russia.

1817 - First coasters with cars that locked to the track. The Aerial Walk became the first full circuit coaster.

1846 – The Centrifugal Railway, Frascati Garden, Paris was the first looping coaster (though it was not a full circuit).

1848 – La Marcus Thompson was born and is commonly referred to as "the Father of the Roller Coaster."

1873 – Mauch Chunk Railway was America's first roller coaster. Built in Pennsylvania, it was the second most visited attraction in America behind Niagara Falls.

1884 – Thompson's Switchback Railway opened at Coney Island in Brooklyn, New York.

1885 - First use of a powered chain lift was on a switchback railway in San Francisco, USA.

1907 - Drop-The-Dips became the first coaster to use lap bar restraints to safely secure passengers.

1920 – The first Golden Age of wooden roller coasters. There were over 2,000 operating rides during this time period.

1925 - Cyclone at Revere Beach, Massachusetts was the first coaster to exceed 100feet in height.

1959 – Matterhorn opened at Disneyland (Anaheim, California) and was the first tubular steel rail coaster and used a modern control system.

1970 – There were only 172 operating roller coasters in the world at this time, down from over 2000 in the 1920s.

1972 – The Racer at Kings Island sparked the Second Golden Age of Wooden roller coasters.

1975 - Corkscrew at Knott's Berry Farm became the first modern looping roller coaster (relocated to Silverwood in 1990).

1976 - First coaster with a modern (clothioid) loop was Revolution at Six Flags Magic Mountain, Valencia California.

1977 – The first launch coaster by means of a weight drop, King Kobra, opened at Kings Dominion in Doswell, Virginia.

1979 – The Beast opened at Kings Island and to this day is still the world's longest wooden roller coaster (7359 feet).

1981 – The first swinging suspended roller coaster, The Bat opened at Kings Island in Mason, Ohio.

1982 – The first coaster to use stand-up trains opened in Japan.

1989 - Magnum Xl-200 at Cedar Point in Sandusky, Ohio became the first full-circuit roller coaster to break the 200-foot barrier.

1992 - First inverted coaster was Batman the Ride at Six Flags Great America in Gurnee, Illinois.

1996 – Flight of Fear at Kings Island was the first to use linear induction motors.

1999 – Hop Hari in San Paolo, Brazil opened South America's first wooden roller coaster.

2000 – Millennium Force at Cedar Point in Sandusky, Ohio became the first full circuit roller coaster to stand over 300 feet tall. It also was the first modern coaster to utilize a cable lift and magnetic brakes. Steel Dragon 2000 (Nagashima Spa Land in Nagashim, Japan) opened and is currently the world's longest roller coaster (8133 feet). Son of Beast at Kings Island is the first modern wooden roller coaster to go upside. It also claimed the record for tallest (218 feet) and fastest (78.4mph) wooden roller coaster ever (the ride was closed in 2009 and demolished in 2012).

2001 – First compressed air launched coaster was Hypersonic XLC at Kings Dominion.

2001 - First 4D coaster, X, opened at Six Flags Magic Mountain.

2002 - Xcelerator at Knotts Berry Farm was the world's first hydraulic launch coaster. Colossus (Thorpe Park in Chertsey, England) was the first roller coaster to feature ten inversions. The Lost Coaster of Superstition Mountain at Indiana Beach is the first wood coaster to use magnetic brakes.

2003 – Top Thrill Dragster, also found at Cedar Point, was the first full-circuit coaster to stand over 400 feet tall.

2005 - Kingda Ka at Six Flags Great Adventure in Jackson, New Jersey opens as the world's tallest roller coaster at 456 feet.

2010 – Formula Rossa at Ferrari World in Abu Dhabi becomes the world's fastest roller coaster at 149.1 mph.

2013 –The Smiler at Alton Towers in the United Kingdom takes the record for most inversions on a coaster with 14. Outlaw Run at Silver Dollar City takes the record for most inversions on a wood coaster with three. The first modern wooden bobsled coaster, Flying Turns, opens at Knoebels in Elysburg, PA.

Present – Currently, there are more than 3,000 roller coasters operating worldwide.

Appendix III: Resources

Websites

American Coaster Enthusiasts (ACE)
http://www.aceonline.org/

ASTM International
http://www.ASTM.org

Amusement Industry Manufacturers and Suppliers (AIMS)
http://www.aimsintl.org/

Amusement Today
http://amusementtoday.com/

Golden Ticket Awards
http://www.goldenticketawards.com/

International Association of Amusement Parks and Aquariums (IAAPA)
http://www.IAAPA.org/

Coaster101
http://www.Coaster101.com

Roller Coaster Database
http://www.RCDB.com

Roller Coaster Physcis
http://www.Rollercoasterphysics.wordpress.com/history

BOOKS

Rutherford, Scott. The American Roller Coaster . MBI. 2000.

Munch, Richard. *Harry G. Traver: Legends of Terror*. Amusement Park Books. 1982.

Coker, Robert. Roller Coasters: A Thrill Seeker's Guide to the Ultimate Scream Machines . Sterling Publishing Co., Inc. 2002

Photography Credits

Pictures by Nick Weisenberger:
Flying Turns at Knoebels
The Beast, Son of Beast, The Racer at Kings Island

Pictures by John Stevenson:
Goliath and Batman: The Ride at Six Flags Great America
Outlaw Run at Silver Dollar City

Pictures by Patrick McGarvey
Magnum XL-200 going over a hill, https://flic.kr/p/6gvGmC
Maverick at Cedar Point

Flickr Pictures distributed under a Cc-BY 2.0 License:
http://creativecommons.org/licenses/by/2.0/

Pictures by Jeremy Thompson:
Holiday World 003, https://flic.kr/p/6nRnMh
Six Flags Great Adventure 008, https://flic.kr/p/cBhRd1
Paramount's Kings Island 1996, https://flic.kr/p/6d8YKb
Disneyland 102, https://flic.kr/p/9bYMWT
Six Flags Magic Mountain 208, https://flic.kr/p/9aQhBc

Vild Svinet (Bonbonland) by Michael Welsing, https://flic.kr/p/4kLJSi
Oblivion by Michael Spiller, https://flic.kr/p/cLpNW
New Texas Giant by Martin Lewison, https://flic.kr/p/fycjTp
NEW Texas Giant Sign by Martin Lewison, https://flic.kr/p/9JzQjA
Giant Dipper by Travis Wise, https://flic.kr/p/pZWSUF
The rides / black and white by João André O. Dias, https://flic.kr/p/dT6XPA
Montezum by Henrique Alves, https://flic.kr/p/8eKPP2
Xcelerator Sunset by Matthew Nelson, https://flic.kr/p/nV4QGN
Cyclone by Doug Letterman, https://flic.kr/p/2ksmPA

Made in the USA
Lexington, KY
17 October 2017